The Field of Drama

Martin Esslin joined the BBC in 1940 and was head of Drama (Radio) from 1963–1977. Currently he lives one half of each year in California, where he is professor of drama at Stanford University, and the other half in London. He is author of books on Pinter, Brecht and Artaud, and of a seminal book on modern drama, *The Theatre of the Absurd*. He has published two collections of essays: *Brief Chronicles: Essays on Modern Drama* and *Mediations: Essays on Brecht, Beckett and the Media*. His critical articles have appeared regularly in *Plays and Players*, *Encounter*, and many other periodicals. He is also a well-known translator of plays, particularly by German-speaking dramatists.

also by Martin Esslin

Brecht: A Choice of Evils
Brecht: After The Wall
Mediations: Essays on Brecht, Beckett and the Media
Pinter the Playwright
The Theatre of The Absurd

MARTIN ESSLIN

The Field of Drama

HOW THE SIGNS OF DRAMA
CREATE MEANING ON STAGE AND SCREEN

Methuen Drama

First published in Great Britain in 1987
by Methuen Publishing Ltd.

First published in paperback 1988

19 20 18

Methuen Drama
A & C Black Publishers Limited
38 Soho Square,
London W1D 3HB

Printed and bound in Great Britain by
MPG Books Ltd, Bodmin, Cornwall

British Library Cataloguing in Publication Data

Esslin, Martin
The field of drama : how the sign of
drama create meaning on stage and screen.
I. Drama. Semiotic aspects
I. Title
808.2

ISBN 978–0–413–19260–8

Contents

All the world's a stage

Shakespeare

El gran teatro del mundo

Calderon

Die Bretter, die die Welt bedeuten

[The boards that signify the world]

Schiller

Wie machen wirs, dass alles frisch und neu
Und mit Bedeutung auch gefällig sei?

[What can we do that all be fresh and new
And with significance be pleasing too?]

Goethe

Preface

There is no shortage of books on the nature and technique of drama. Yet I have always been struck by the narrowness of their scope: they tend to concentrate entirely on stage drama, when, in fact, the overwhelming majority of dramatic material, the largest proportion of the actual experience of drama for the vast millions of its public, is derived from drama in the cinema and, above all, in television.

The specialists, whether theoreticians of classical tragedy or highly sophisticated film critics – there is as yet hardly any serious criticism of drama on television – regard their respective areas as strictly separate. Yet the ordinary member of the public does not make these rigid distinctions. That great and highly intelligent actress Elisabeth Bergner once told me that she had at last persuaded Albert Einstein, who was a great friend and admirer of hers, to accompany her to the theatre. After the performance she asked him what he had thought of the play. But the great man refused to give an opinion. He knew too little about the finer points of performance. 'You see', he said, 'I hardly ever go to the cinema!'.

To look at the whole 'field of drama' seems to me to be a useful undertaking, precisely because only by starting from an overview of all the aspects of dramatic performance can we arrive at a clear differentiation of those features that each of the separate media – stage, film and television – can claim as specifically their own, as against the much larger number of aspects they have in common.

I have also always thought it absurd that the rigid separation of stage drama from the cinematic media in higher education has led to the creation of separate theatre and film departments in most universities and colleges, often hardly communicating with each other when each could greatly profit from sharing their insights into what, basically, are closely related and sometimes identical areas of theory and practice, which could much more effectively be covered in a unified performing arts department.

Moreover, in recent times, important new ideas have been applied to the analysis of drama, the way in which it achieves its effects and conveys its meaning. This *semiotic* approach is, basically, extremely simple and practical. It asks: how is it done? and tries to supply the most down-to-earth answers, by examining the *signs* that are used to achieve the desired communication.

There is, of course, nothing radically new here, except that the enterprise is systematic and methodical rather than ad-hoc and impressionistic. When I first came across the beginnings of the new scholarly literature on the *semiology* and *semiotics* of the theatre and film I felt rather like Molière's M. Jourdain who was surprised to discover that he had been talking 'prose' all his life. For in my practical work as a director of drama these were precisely the questions that had always occupied me in making the innumerable practical choices which constitute the work of a director: what kind of costume should this character wear? should he sit or stand while speaking these lines? if I cut this speech what element of meaning will be lost?

To approach dramatic performance as an enterprise involving the use of a large number of signs and sign-systems and to clarify the role each of these elements plays in creating the ultimate meaning of the performance thus clearly is an extremely serviceable and helpful tool both for the practitioner of drama and the member of the public who wants to be critically aware of what he has been seeing and experiencing.

What struck me as unfortunate, however, from the outset, was the obscure language and excessively abstract way in which the, in many cases, outstandingly brilliant exponents of semiotics presented their findings. It almost seemed as though the very practicality and down-to-earth concreteness of what they were basically engaged in had led them to try and make it appear as 'scientific' and 'philosophical' as possible. Of course, a scholarly subject needs a precise vocabulary. But all too often, in reading these very involved texts, I for one was forced to translate them back into practical terms only to realise that a very simple fact had been clothed in the most involved language.

I well remember a conference on the semiotics of drama I attended to which one of the most distinguished directors of one of the world's leading theatres had been invited. The assembled scholars delivered themselves of their respective, highly intelligent and theoretically brilliant papers, and then, eagerly asked the famous practitioner whether he had found some insights for his own work. They were deeply disappointed when he told them that he had found it all wholly useless and impenetrable.

That, I think, is really unfortunate. For a semiotic approach, provided it is expressed in intelligible language, could be of great help to directors, designers, actors and other practitioners of drama on stage and screen. It could, even at the most basic level, lead them to think more clearly about what they are doing intuitively and by instinct.

Hence the present attempt to provide an overview of the field of drama, seen in the light of semiotics but in the widest possible general frame of reference, in a form that might be accessible both to the practical workers in that field and to the general public of drama in all its forms.

I have tried to avoid, as much as that is possible, the proliferation of obscure vocabulary and pseudo-scientific jargon that screens so much valuable insight from the non-specialists. And I have always made my experience as a practical director, dramaturg and critic the final arbiter in enunciating any principles or conclusions. That – the constant testing of the theory against actual results – seems to me the real use of a genuinely 'scientific' methodology.

To make the book as accessible as possible to practical workers and students in drama, I have tried to restrict the number of foot-notes and needless polemics with the specialist literature, but, on the other hand, to provide a fairly full bibliography of the whole field.

This book started as a series of lectures I was asked to give at the University of California, Santa Barbara, and I am greatly indebted to Professor H. Porter Abbott and Professor Paul Hernadi whose initiative and help made it possible.

I am also grateful to my students who attended a graduate seminar I gave in the semiotics of drama at Stanford and whose critical contributions to the discussion did much to clarify some of my ideas.

My friend Archana Horsting contributed valuable comments and ideas. Mr Peter Luddington, of Grant & Cutler Ltd., London, enabled me to obtain books on the subject in a number of languages – there are few bookshops left in the world capable of giving such truly scholarly bibliographical assistance.

And my special thanks are due to Mr Nicholas Hern of Methuen's, as editor of rare expertise and patience.

Martin Esslin

Winchelsea, Sussex
August 1986

I

Introduction

I

Drama, there can be no doubt about it, has become immensely important in our time. More human beings than ever before see more drama than ever before and are more directly influenced, conditioned, programmed by drama than ever before. Drama has become one of the principal vehicles of information, one of the prevailing methods of 'thinking' about life and its situations.

Our time has witnessed a veritable explosion of drama through the photographic and electronic mass media. Where, previously, stage drama, live theatre, was the only method for the communication of dramatic performance, today dramatic performance can reach its audiences in a multitude of ways: through the cinema, television, videotape, radio, cassette-recordings. Consequently not only has the *audience* for drama increased by truly astronomical progression as compared to previous ages, the actual *quantity* of dramatic performances produced has gone up in equal proportion.

Hence the immensely increased importance of drama in the life and culture of our time: never before has drama been so pervasive in the lives of the large masses of people. Gone are the days when experience of a dramatic performance was either a rare feast-day occurrence; or restricted to the social elites of courts; or accessible only to the more affluent classes in the larger cities. Drama has become one of the principal means of communication of ideas and, even more importantly, modes of human behaviour in our civilisation: drama provides some of the principal role models by which individuals form their identity and ideals, sets patterns of communal behaviour, forms values and aspirations, and has become part of the collective fantasy life of the masses – with the adventures of the heroes of television series, the comic characters of situation comedy, the powerful demi-gods of the cinema taking the place occupied by the heroes of the popular culture, folklore and myth of previous ages.

More than ever, therefore, there is a need for us to understand what drama can and cannot express, how it formulates and transmits its messages, what techniques it employs to convey them to its audience and how that audience can and does grasp, ingest and understand the *meaning* of these messages – explicit or implicit, consciously understood or subliminally absorbed.

That is why it should be worthwhile to attempt to look, in the light of the fundamental technological changes of the last hundred years and their impact on dramatic performance in its traditional and its new media of transmission, upon the whole *field of drama*:

What are the means by which drama achieves its impact? Which of these are employed, in common, by all the various dramatic media? And which are specific to one or several among them? In what ways do the effects of the different dramatic media upon their audiences vary, and why? And – how do they mutually influence, how can they learn from, each other?

From the very beginnings of theoretical thinking about the ways drama achieves its effects the question of how drama works its effects has been approached in a severely practical manner: Aristotle's *Poetics* (the most influential theoretical work about drama in its whole long history) derives its conclusions, which have often assumed the authority of unbreakable rules, from considerations of what kinds of actions, what kinds of characters would exercise the most powerful emotional effect upon an audience. The famous rules about the unities of time, place and action derive from the assumption that, for example, people sitting in a theatre would find it difficult to believe that the stage could represent different locations within the span of a single play, lasting an hour; and that, similarly, they would find it impossible to credit an action unfolding itself within that hour as comprising events occurring over months or years, that, in fact, the most they could accept would be the compression of the events of a single day into that hour.

Our own experience has shown that these assumptions by Aristotle, which dominated the practice of drama in so many places for such long periods are incorrect, at least as far as present-day audiences are concerned, although it may, indeed, well be that they were wholly valid for spectators in Aristotle's own time. We must never forget that human capacities can change through time: human beings may learn to adjust themselves to new ways of perception, to increase their speed of reaction, and gain practice in accepting new ways of seeing and experiencing both reality and art. Children growing up nowadays who see several hours of drama on television each day must be infinitely more effectively conditioned to accept and understand dramatic conventions than earlier populations who may have had far fewer opportunities to experience dramatic performance.

Yet, if Aristotle's approach was based on practical considerations, dramatic criticism has, in the course of time, also frequently succumbed to the temptations of becoming all too abstract, of slavishly following authorities of the past (above all Aristotle's *Poetics* themselves, having become hardened into rigid dogma), excessively divorced from the practice of the art and, even more dangerously, of growing excessively theoretical. More attention, for example, was, at one time, devoted to the analysis of, say, the characters of Shakespeare, as though they were real people, than to the more mundane problem of how Shakespeare actually delineated character. This, ultimately, amounted, and still amounts, to a concentration on the *content* of drama (important though that clearly is) rather than on the *means* and *methods* by which drama conveys its contents. Yet the dichotomy between content and form is a false one, because form determines content and content form and a change of form alters the content, and a change of content requires a different form to express it. And so, to neglect a closer analysis of the often very mundane methods by which meaning is conveyed in drama is to inhibit an understanding in depth of the essential considerations upon which truly insightful – and constructive – criticism must be based.

All the elements of a dramatic performance – the language of the dialogue, the setting, the gestures, costumes, make-up and voice-inflections of the actors, as well as a multitude of other signs – each in their own way contribute to the creation of the 'meaning' of the performance. A dramatic performance must, at the most basic level, be regarded as essentially a process by which information about the actions that are to be mimetically reproduced is conveyed to the audience. Each element of the performance can be regarded as a sign that stands for an ingredient of the over-all meaning of a scene, an incident, a moment of the action.

Ever since the Middle Ages attempts have been made to explore and systematize our understanding of how signs work. In the last half century these efforts have been intensified in the creation of the discipline of Semiotics, the branch of knowledge that deals with signs and how signs are used in communication between human beings to convey meaning.

By approaching the dramatic media with some of the methods and tools that Semiotics has made available we can open up a down-to-earth, highly practical and concrete approach to the understanding and critical appreciation of drama. By examining by what means, what signs, drama conveys the basic information through which the dramatic fiction is built up, piece by piece, and through which the characters, the time and place of the action, the events which form its 'plot' are delineated, a semiotic approach can shed valuable light on the process of how an audience comes to apprehend the basic outline of the dramatic action, the very ground from which the complex and multifarious higher levels of meaning of the performance will ultimately arise for the audience.

There has been a great upsurge of interest and research in the semiotics of theatre in recent years and much valuable work has been done by a number of semioticians, above all in France, Germany and Italy. The present study proposes to make use of their results, but to maintain, at the same time, a certain critical distance from their methods and aims.

2

The semiotics of drama in its present form originated at the beginning of this century – from the work of the Russian formalist critics who began to develop ways of looking at the formal aspects of works of literature by close analysis of how they are actually producing their effects; followers of this tendency, largely in Prague in the 1930s, began to apply this method to drama. They were, at the same time, also inspired by the work of the two great pioneers of the new approach that has been the basis of the current development of semiotics: Ferdinand de Saussure (1857–1913), the father of modern linguistics, (whose 'Course in General Linguistics' was reconstructed from their lecture notes and posthumously published by some of his pupils in 1916), and the great American philosopher Charles S. Peirce (1839–1914).

Saussure treated language as a system of signs – and both he and Peirce then extended the idea by pointing out that, in fact, language is just one, among many, systems of signs – pictures, gestures, manners, movements, and a whole host of others – and that, to understand how human beings communicate about the world and themselves, an analysis of *all* these different systems of signs would be useful and productive. That field of analysis is semiology, its body of knowledge – semiotics.

If we look at a work of art, semioticians argue, as an act of communication among human beings and if we can analyse the actual process by which this communication takes place, we might arrive at a more thorough and perhaps more objective method of talking about works of art – through an analysis of what actually happens between the originator of the communication and its recipient. If a play or a dramatic work of cinema or television produces certain effects, insights or emotions in a member of the audience: what has actually taken place? And how was it brought about? By which signs and signals was its meaning evoked in the minds of its audience?

Where, in my opinion, the more fanatical adherents of this methodology in the field of drama go too far, is their assumption that by using a methodology analogous to that of linguistics it would be possible to produce something akin to an exact science, grammar and syntax of signification in drama. At one time it was felt by some of the more dedicated semioticians of the theatre that it would be possible to capture the totality of a dramatic performance by listing all the separate signifiers that produce meaning at any given moment, or 'beat', of the production and thus arrive at a notation that would be analogous to the full orchestral score of a symphony.

These attempts have by now been considerably scaled down by some of the most ambitious and gifted exponents of the idea. As one of these, the brilliant French semiotician Patrice Pavis put it as early as 1980:

> Il y a à peine dix ans, il n'était pas incongru de poser la question – devenue entre temps rhétorique – de la possibilité d'une sémiologie du théâtre. C'était le temps (o nostalgie!) des raids nocturnes en territoire linguistique et du bricolage clandestin de modèles empruntés aux sciences du langage. . . .
> [Hardly ten years ago it seemed not incongruous to ask the question – which has since become rhetorical – about the

> possibility of a semiology of theatre. That was the time (o nostalgia!) of nocturnal raids into linguistic territory and of clandestine tinkering with models borrowed from linguistic science. . .][1]

The idea that the theatre – and by extension drama – being a system of signs could be treated as a language with its own grammar and syntax and with the scientific rigour with which linguistics tackles verbal languages turned out to have been a misleading analogy, simply because of the complexity of dramatic performance, where a very large number of signifiers are simultaneously unleashed upon the audience in the course of the performance, with the additional difficulty that some of these, like the elements of the setting (a room, its furniture) persist relatively unchanged throughout a whole scene or act, while others (the inflections of speech, the gestures and facial expressions of the characters) change from moment to moment. This makes it almost impossible to arrive at a basic unit – analogous to the basic unit of meaning (a *semanteme* in linguistics or a bar in the notation of music) by which the multitude of signifiers unleashed upon the audience could be noted down for any given moment of the performance. Moreover, even if this were possible, so great is the number of different elements that contribute, for the individual spectator, to the 'meaning' of the performance at any given moment, that it is quite impossible to determine which of these he or she would actually perceive, consciously or even subliminally, and what importance he or she would attribute to them in what order of priorities. While at a given moment one spectator might be enthralled by a phrase of poetry, another might be absorbed by contemplating the costume of the actress uttering those words, or noticing the reaction of another character to the same speech.

For it is a characteristic of all complex media of communication that the numerous bits of information they convey are

[1] Patrice Pavis, *Voix et Images de la Scène*, Lille: Presses Universitaires de Lille, 2nd end. 1985, p. 9.

taken in partly on a conscious level and at the same time also partly subliminally. Elements of costume or decor that are not consciously noticed might contribute to the creation, in the mind of an individual spectator, of atmosphere, mood and other highly important aspects of the experience. After all: in our perception of situations which confront us in 'real' life, we are also constantly responding to elements of mood, atmosphere and other subliminally absorbed impressions that underlie the consciously perceived elements of our experience. A room we enter, a person we meet, evokes a reaction compounded of a multitude of such elements. The external world is intuitively perceived by us through a multitude of associations and connotations determined by our past experience, memories, habits and conditioning. Drama represents this external world and is largely perceived in the same intuitive fashion.

There is an additional factor which makes too close an analogy between the workings of language and those of drama questionable. In purely verbal communication the intention of the speaker can be more or less readily ascertained. A dramatic performance, on the other hand, unlike linguistic utterance and, indeed, the products of most other arts, is never the work of a single individual, mirroring a single individual's intention to communicate. Neither the author, nor the director, however masterly their effort at co-ordinating the work of the team, can ever be wholly in control of the total product, the ultimate meaning of the 'message' that reaches the spectator. Deliberately, or unintentionally, the work, say of the costume designer, might be in dialectical conflict with, say, the creator of the make-up. And the resultant consonance or dissonance of these elements must necessarily vibrate in different ways in the consciousness, or subliminal perception, of individual spectators.

What this amounts to is that dramatic performance, whatever its originators have intended by their selection of the meaning-creating elements they have put into it (and they will inevitably also have provided some which they did not consciously plan to include) must, with its plethora of signifiers, be widely 'over-determined' for every individual spectator. And any attempt to predict what 'meaning' the performance as such contains, is bound to be doomed to failure, simply because that meaning must be different for each individual member of the audience. Also, however well designed all these elements may be, their effectiveness will depend on the abilities of the company: a bad actor will lessen the significance of his speeches.

These are some of the reservations with which the methodology and body of knowledge already made available by semiotics have to be approached. Another aspect of the matter is the desire of some of the pioneers in this field to evolve a vocabulary that would to the initiated and uninitiated alike be a sign that they are in the presence of an exact science. The jargon of semiotics, analysed by the methods of semiotics, must be seen as signifying: 'this is serious, exact, scientific stuff'. As a result many insights that are mere truisms appear in the semiotic jargon like profound and esoteric discoveries in hitherto unexplored realms of knowledge. Nothing is more apt to discredit the truly useful and valuable insights of semiotics in the eyes of the practitioners of drama than such pretentious use of language.

These considerations notwithstanding, semiotics provides a most valuable method for a better understanding of the way dramatic performance creates its mimesis of human interaction through setting before its audience a duplicate, mimetic, illusionary image of the world in all its complexity.

What then are the delimitations of the field of drama, and what is its essential nature?

II

The Field of Drama

'... I have heard
That guilty creatures, sitting at a play
Have by the very cunning of the scene
Been struck so to the soul that presently
They have proclaim'd their malefactions ...'

Hamlet, II, ii

I

The 'scene', the 'play', the whole gamut of staged events that fall under the description of 'drama' can, indeed, not only help us to pass the time agreeably but provide us with strong emotional experiences, 'strike us to our soul' and produce powerful effects upon our lives, our thinking, our behaviour.

How, by what devices, by what methods, *does* the scene exercise its cunning? How does drama exert its impact upon the creatures – guilty or innocent – who come to be entertained or moved by what Hamlet calls 'but ... a fiction, ... a dream of passion': a dramatic performance?

It is a question that has exercised theorists and critics of drama for almost three millennia and has evoked a wide variety of answers, more or less valid, more or less applicable in the flux of ever-changing cultural, social and technological conditions under which drama has been produced and performed.

That is why the question must be re-formulated and posed again. The conditions under which drama is presented have been radically transformed in the last hundred years by a veritable flood of technological innovation: on the stage itself, and later by the introduction of mechanical and electronic diffusion.

What is drama and where are the boundaries of its field? Rigid definitions of highly variable and constantly developing, organically growing and decaying, human activities of this nature are dangerous. As Wittgenstein puts it:

> 'many words. . . . don't have a strict meaning. But this is no defect. To think it is would be like saying that the light of my reading lamp is not a real light because it has no sharp boundary.'[1]

Definitions of concepts like 'drama' should, therefore, never be treated as normative, but as merely outlining the somewhat fluid boundaries of a given field. Whenever narrow, normative definitions dominated the practice of drama, they invariably tended to have a cramping and deadening impact.

The history of drama (which for so long was almost synonymous with the history of theatre) is rich in examples of such a negative effect of over-rigid definitions. Like Wittgenstein's light, the concept of 'drama' has an obvious, immediately recognised, central core, which can, if not defined, be described and circumscribed, but will always be surrounded by a penumbra of events and activities which, while partaking of some of its characteristics, will to some extent lack others. Thus mime, the circus, street theatre, opera, music hall, cabaret, 'happenings', performance art fall within the boundaries of the dramatic while lacking some of the elements of stricter definitions of drama. The boundaries of the term will always be fluid, the different related fields will always tend to overlap. Nevertheless the concept has a centre that is common to all its multifarious overlapping manifestations. How can we delimit it? We use the terms 'drama' and 'dramatic' in a multitude of contexts: a football match, a race, a riot, an assassination are 'dramatic' because they contain the elements of heightened intensity of incident and emotion that are one of the essential ingredients of

[1] Wittgenstein, *The Blue and Brown Books*, Oxford: Blackwell, 1958, p. 27.

drama. What distinguishes them from drama in its proper sense is that they are 'real' rather than fictional. So the element of the fictional is an essential element of drama? Only up to a point, for there is also 'documentary drama', based on 'real' events. The essential element here is that the documentary drama 're-enacts' past events, that is: puts them before an audience as though they were happening before them at that very moment.

This brings out one of the essential aspects of drama: the aspect of 'acting'. Drama simulates, enacts or re-enacts events that have, or may be imagined to have, happened in the 'real' or in an imagined world. What these different types of representation have in common is that they are all 'mimetic action'.

A dramatic text is a blueprint for such mimetic action, it is not yet itself, in the full sense, drama. A dramatic text, unperformed, is literature. It can be read as a story. This is the area where the fields of narrative fiction, epic poetry, and drama overlap. The element which distinguishes drama from these types of fiction is, precisely, that of 'performance', *enactment*. Dickens giving readings from his novels, in some sense acted them out, and thus transformed them into drama. Clearly his vocal characterisation of his fruity and highly individualised characters amounted to 'acting'. And as to the purely narrative, descriptive, dialogue-free portions of the text: Dickens, in reading these, in a highly emotional and subtly differentiated voice that painted the mood and the scenery, was still an actor: he acted the role of the character 'Charles Dickens', the compulsive story-teller; he played an obsessed individual who, like the Ancient Mariner, grabs his listener and does not let him escape from the telling of his tale. Such narrations, acted out in character, have always been an important ingredient of drama. The messengers of Greek tragedy, after all, were also merely *narrating* events, describing them as a novelist would, though 'in character'. And, indeed, the bard who sang his heroic poems at the table of Homeric princes (including Homer himself, no doubt) gave a dramatic performance. And it was out of such enacted epic narrations inserted into choral religious song that drama proper seems to have originated and evolved in ancient Greece.

Dramatic reading of narrative texts has revived in our time on radio and in cassette recordings. And probably under the influence of such dramatic readings on radio the acted performance of narrative material on the stage has become popular and widespread: the American forms of 'story theatre' fall under this heading, so do the numerous solo performances by star-actors of the works of writers of narrative, diaries or letters. Emlyn Williams re-enacted Dickens reading from his novels; Roy Dotrice transformed Aubrey's *Brief Lives* into a character cameo of that quirky old eccentric telling his anecdotes. The genre has become ubiquitous. What this demonstrates is the essential difference between the narrative and the dramatic mode: the narrative, when read is perceived as lying in the *past*, the dramatic, as Goethe and Schiller pointed out in their classic discussion of the matter, creates an eternal *present*: in this case a narrator present in the room telling his story here and now becomes – re-enacts himself as – a character.

In the case of the modern novel, where the omniscient narrator has been replaced by an individualised character who tells the story from his viewpoint, the dividing line between a dramatic text and narrative fiction has become equally tenuous: Beckett's 'novels' are in fact dramatic monologues that differ only very slightly from the dramatic monologues that are published as his 'plays'. They can be performed without changing the words.

At the other end of the spectrum there is the novel that reduces the narrator to a minimum and is mainly composed of dialogues, like the work of Ivy Compton-Burnett. Such novels can also be 'performed' with minimal changes of their text.

And, if we approach the fluid boundary between narrative fiction and drama from the opposite direction: there is Brecht's 'epic theatre' which endeavours to import the detachment, the critical, 'historical' viewpoint of the epic poem and the novel into dramatic performance, so that the audience should be enabled to see the action with the detachment, the distanced analytical eye and critical mind of the reader of a novel, or historical narrative, as though it was *not* happening 'here and now' but 'there and then'.

If the boundaries between fiction and 'mimesis' are fluid, they are equally so at the other end of the spectrum, that of non-fictional 'action' or 'events': Renaissance *triomfi*; elaborate Corpus Christi processions in Bavaria, Austria or Belgium, involving huge puppets parading through the streets (and revived by Peter Schumann's Bread and Puppet theatre); carnival processions and parades with floats depicting scenes and characters; pageants; masked balls in which individuals are costumed as Nubian slaves or pirates; the circus with animal acts, jugglers, high-wire and trapeze artistes and clowns, glitter and costume, evoking the excitement of intense emotion are all very closely akin to that of drama more rigidly defined. Pageantry of all kinds involves the highly dramatic element of *spectacle*: the military parade or religious procession is something to be looked at in awe and wonder – gorgeous uniforms, spectacular vestments share with drama 'proper' the element of costume and spectacular grouping of characters; religious processions and *triomfi* also used 'floats' which can be regarded as mobile stages on which 'tableaux' of mythological or religious character were displayed (as do contemporary carnival processions or the London 'Lord Mayor's parade'). Masked balls are often held in halls that have been turned into elaborate stage sets and the participants are not only costumed as 'characters' they also tend to want to improvise dialogue and actions appropriate to their dress – in other words turn themselves into 'actors'. Circus artists (such as bare-back-riders, jugglers, trapeze artistes, acrobats, tight-rope-walkers) do not appear as 'fictional' characters, yet their glittering costumes make them figures of fantasy; nor must one forget that the display of physical skills and physical beauty is an important part of dramatic performance itself – great actors often excel by their beauty and physical prowess as well as by other qualities.

(And, indeed, circus and theatre have frequently overlapped: the English pantomime includes jugglers and other circus-like elements; plays and films have occasionally relied on the spectacular feats of trained animals: Goethe relinquished his post as the director of the Weimar theatre in 1817 because he objected to the court's insistence that he put on a play that included the feats of a trained poodle[2], a forerunner of the cinema's Rin-Tin-Tin and Lassie; the early cinema also derived much of its attraction from the really or seemingly dangerous feats of daring rough riders and actors who jumped from moving trains, or hung suspended from sky-scrapers like Harold Lloyd.)

Contemporary avant-garde performance art, environmental theatre, 'happenings' and similar experimental works derive in many ways from these traditions of pageantry: here too often the performers remain themselves, or do not attempt to turn themselves into fictional characters, yet the 'images' they create, or the way in which they transform the audience into participants of improvised dialogue are clearly well within the boundaries of the 'dramatic'. One need only mention practitioners like the 'Living Theatre' of the sixties and seventies, Robert Wilson, Ariane Mnouchkine, Luca Ronconi in this context.

And then, at yet another boundary of the field of drama, there are the highly ritualised spectacular ceremonials involving kings and queens and other political figure-heads, like the 'Trooping of the Colour' in Britain, the vast military parades in front of Lenin's tomb, the inauguration of the President of the United States.

[2] The play was a French thriller *Der Hund des Aubri de Mont-Didier* with which the Viennese actor Karsten was touring Germany. See Marvin Carlson, *Goethe and the Weimar Theatre*, Ithaca and London: Cornell University Press, 1978, p. 288 ff.

Closely akin to the vast field of drama and sharing and overlapping its boundaries there is the equally immense field of religious ritual (historically so closely related to the origins of drama itself) which frequently not only involves spectacular 'action' but also includes a strong 'mimetic' element, as the re-enactment of Christ's archetypal handling of bread and wine, in a variety of more or less symbolic forms, in the Eucharist. If, from these boundaries of the concept, we return to its central core, we can perhaps sum it up as consisting of: mimetic action, in the sense of the re-enactment of 'real' or fictional events, involving the actions and interaction of human beings, real or simulated (e.g. puppets or cartoon characters) before an audience as though they were happening at that very moment.

The audience is an essential ingredient here. Even a rehearsal has an audience: the director or, indeed, the actors themselves, who are observing the evolution and effectiveness of their own performance, in order to shape or improve it further.

The artist who performs the mimetic action, the actor, thus stands at the very centre of the art of drama. The art form truly specific to drama is the art of acting. But drama also can and does use all the other arts: painting, sculpture and architecture to represent the environment, music to provide mood, rhythm – and indeed to represent the practice of music (people shown singing or dancing within the context of the world that is being represented) and of course 'literature' in the widest sense, for its verbal element. In drawing on the other arts and fusing them into a new whole, drama thus is the most hybrid (if we look at it in a purist spirit) or the most complete synthesis of all the arts: what Richard Wagner called the Gesamtkunstwerk – the 'total work of art'.

Where, then, are the boundaries of the field of drama?

2

A filmed version of a stage play, whether by Pinter or Shakespeare, clearly is still drama. But is a film based on an original screenplay drama? Or a situation comedy on television? Or the circus? Is a musical play drama? And if so, is opera drama? Or ballet? Or the puppet theatre? I, for one, am convinced that all these different forms of 'art' or 'entertainment' *are* essentially drama, or at least contain an important ingredient of 'the dramatic'.

Drama is unique among the representational arts in that it represents 'reality' by using real human beings and often also real objects, to create its fictional universe. A fictitious young man – say Romeo – is depicted by a 'real' young man. A fictional chair in the house of John Gabriel Borkman or in the palace of Elsinore is represented by a chair that you might have in your own house. In this particular respect human beings themselves appear as objects in the picture: in a painting a chair would be represented by strokes of the brush on canvas, so would the young man called Hamlet. In a piece of literary fiction both would be represented by words that appear as black imprints on white paper. In drama, fiction is created by using 'real' human beings, 'real' objects to evoke the illusion of a fictional world. But these real elements can be combined with any imaginable means to create illusion. The square in Verona (on which a real young man, representing the fictional Romeo, dressed in 'real clothes' uses a 'real' sword to fight with with another 'real' young man, representing the fictional Tybalt), might be represented by a painted backdrop. Yet again, if we think of a filmed version of *Romeo and Juliet*, that square in Verona might be represented by patterns of light thrown onto a screen which forms a photographic image of a real piazza in Verona. . . .

For if the outline of the central essentials of the concept of drama that I have attempted is correct a filmed version of Romeo and Juliet is still drama – and hence the cinema of fictional subjects must also fall under the general category of dramatic art. And if there is a television version of *Romeo and Juliet* clearly that also is a specimen of dramatic art – however different the specific techniques and technologies of that particular medium of transmission might be.

Indeed: to be able to think clearly about how drama in all its different media of transmission works, it seems to me, it is important to be able to recognise the essential features that are present in stage, cinematic, television (and perhaps radio) drama so as to be in a position to explore, equally clearly and usefully, the technical, technological and psychological differences that arise from the different modes of conveying those essential dramatic features to their recipients: the public of stage, cinema, television (and perhaps radio[3]).

This may appear as outrageous heresy to those purists of the

[3] I have put radio in brackets because, although radio drama also is undoubtedly drama, it has some paradoxical and complex features. Clearly radio drama is also mimetic action, it is performed by actors, who have to be as skilled and indeed in some respects more skilled than the actors in the cinema, television or on the stage. And if, as will appear in the subsequent discussion, drama unfolds in both time and space, so does radio drama: the acoustics in which the action occurs and the perspectives that place the voices at different distances and angles from the microphone – and hence the listener – in radio drama also contain an enormously strong suggestion of space. What radio drama lacks is a 'visual' dimension. Yet experience with listeners to radio drama shows that even this dimension is present, simply because the performance in time and acoustic space very strongly conjures up visual images. It has been argued that in this respect radio drama is even more satisfying than those forms of drama that contain palpable visuals. If the heroine of a play is described as the most beautiful woman who ever lived, each listener produces his own ideal image – something that no actress physically present could do for all spectators. Similarly the noise of a battle can evoke a more satisfying visual image in the mind of the listener than even the most spectacular filmed scene.

While many of the visual aspects of drama are also present in radio, its inclusion in the discussion of the many visual aspects of drama on stage and screen might unduly complicate matters. Hence I have opted for excluding radio drama from the main body of the book. Readers, interested in this form of drama, might well apply its conclusions 'mutatis mutandis' to it.

cinema who are still insisting on the total distinctness of the 'seventh art' from all the others, and in particular from the theatre. That the theatre (live, staged drama) is *sui generis* and distinct in many of its methods from the cinema (and the cinematic forms of television) is, of course, beyond doubt. Equally, however, it seems to me beyond doubt that common to both of them is the underlying ground upon both of which ultimately stand, the ground of *drama*.

This is, more or less explicitly – and often merely implicitly – acknowledged by most serious theoreticians and critics of the cinema today, although in practice cinema criticism is treated by them as a wholly distinct field with its own vocabulary and conceptual apparatus. It is the contention of this book that this division has become somewhat of an anachronism and inhibits clear critical thinking about the very considerable number of essential and fundamental aspects that the dramatic media have in common.

Historically the insistence of serious film criticism, from its very inception, on the distinctness of the cinema as an art form, derived, quite naturally, from the rejection of the original naive assumption on the part of the earliest distributors (and producers) of cinema that it was, like the phonograph, merely a mechanical means for reproducing (and, as it were, 'canning') theatre performances. Hence the increasing emphasis of the pioneers of film aesthetics on the profound differences between theatre and cinema and their insistence on the narrative, epic quality of the cinema which made it more akin to the novel than to drama in the theatre; and, above all, on its distinct 'language' of montage, editing, panning and travelling shots etc. This led, naturally, to an almost total neglect, in the more elevated regions of film aesthetics and film criticism, of such qualities as the level of the language of the dialogue, the contribution of the actors (the emotional effect of acting being capable of being manipulated by montage), designers of sets and costume, etc. And this division was enshrined, in the terminology of film aesthetics, in the dichotomy between 'mise-en-scène' (i.e. the spectacle that was filmed) and 'film direction' (i.e. the way the director decided to film it and assemble its fragments in a meaningful sequence).

Criticism of all aspects of mise-en-scène thus became a neglected step-child of film aesthetics. The great pioneers in the field, Arnheim, Eisenstein, Kracauer concentrated on the specific qualities of photography, montage, viewpoint etc., and their successors also tended, and still tend, to deal with the specifically 'filmic' elements, which, in fact, often means exclusively the work of the director as the guiding influence on the choice of shots and ultimate assembler of their sequence. Hence the evolution of the 'auteur theory' of film, which elevates the director to the position of the 'sole begetter' of his film, a theory which quite obviously neglects many decisive elements of the practical, financial and sociological infrastructure of actual film production: however powerful the influence of the director on the choice of subject matter, casting or the script, the producer, the cinematographer, the actors, the designers, the make-up artists, the scriptwriters and a whole host of other creative and practical contributors, clearly also often have a decisive part in the final, collective product: the finished film. And the contributions of many of these fall within an area that they share with other dramatic media: acting, costume, props, furniture design, make-up, music, dialogue, dance etc., etc.

A close reading of the works of the outstanding critics in this field, such as Metz, Mitry, Bazin, shows that, in fact, by implication they also recognise the underlying category of the 'dramatic' which is the ultimate objective of the whole enterprise of making a film for an audience: the evocation in human beings of laughter, pity and fear, compassion, vicarious experience of the whole gamut of emotions and sentiments and that ultimate 'catharsis' of which Aristotle spoke in his *Poetics*.

In his important articles on 'Theatre and Cinema' (1951) the doyen of modern film criticism André Bazin, for example, talks about the fact that early slapstick film comedies represented

> 'the rebirth of dramatic forms that had practically disappeared, such as farce and the *Commedia dell'Arte*. Certain dramatic situations, certain techniques that had degenerated in the course of time, found again, in the cinema, first the sociological nourishment they needed to survive and, still better, the conditions favourable to an expansive use of their aesthetic, which the theatre had kept congenitally atrophied'[4]

With even greater clarity Bazin speaks, in the same important essay, of the 'dramatic element' as 'interchangeable between one art and another'.[5]

It thus seems legitimate to attempt an examination of the whole field of drama. That is: to try and describe the ways, common to all the dramatic media, by which they achieve their peculiarly 'dramatic' effects, i.e. those effects that derive from the mimesis of human interaction through its embodiment by human beings assuming the identities of (fictional or real but 'historical') human beings and presenting this interaction to an audience, as though it was happening at that very moment before their own eyes.

Such an examination of the expressive elements (the language of the signs employed to convey the action, and the 'grammar' of this 'language') which are used by all the dramatic media, would also make it easier to discuss and determine the ways in which the dramatic media *differ* from each other, that is: which elements of their language they do *not* share with one or several of the others and that thus are peculiar to each of them.

In other words: a study of the workings of drama starting from its central core, (all the expressive means that are used by

[4] André Bazin, *What is Cinema? Essays selected and translated by Hugh Gray*, vol I, Berkeley, Los Angeles and London: University of California Press, 1967, p. 121.
[5] op.cit. p. 115.

the different dramatic media), and then moving outwards from the shared common core in divergent directions towards the specific methods peculiar to only one or two of them, might considerably help to clarify the process of rational criticism of the whole field as well as its sub-divisions.

Quite apart from any other considerations such an approach might also have an important impact on the way drama is taught in *theory*, and on the ways its *practitioners* are trained in the techniques of their craft. The exclusive concentration on stage drama, and in particular on the written texts of plays, in the drama departments of universities seems to me a relic of the past, when the live theatre really was, for century after century, the sole medium of transmission for drama. And similarly film departments of colleges and universities and practical film schools tend to neglect many of the basic dramatic elements of the cinema.

After all: in the real world the practitioners of drama have not made and do not make these rigid distinctions: Chaplin, Keaton, W. C. Fields and the Marx Brothers came from the music hall and vaudeville (clearly branches of popular theatre), Orson Welles from avant-garde theatre; Artaud had ambitions as a screen writer; Cocteau wrote stage plays and ballets as well as writing and directing films; Laurence Olivier started as a man of the stage, and so did a whole host of the best screen actors; Samuel Beckett writes television (and radio) plays; Bertolt Brecht laboured as a screenwriter in Hollywood; Harold Pinter is one of the best screenwriters (and radio dramatists) in the world; one of Ingmar Bergman's greatest films, *The Seventh Seal*, was an adaptation of a radio play he had written; Rainer Werner Fassbinder oscillated between writing and directing for avant-garde theatres in the cellars of Munich and multimillion dollar films; the same texts appear, more or less lightly adapted, in all the dramatic media; many leading actors tend to be prominent in all of them; many of the best directors and designers work in the theatre, film and television and can switch from one to the other without undue difficulty. And, in my experience, they regard their work in all the different dramatic media as basically the exercise of a single type of skill that can be readily adapted to the specific differences and demands of the different media.

III

The Nature of Drama

I

When the great eighteenth-century German critic and theoretician, Lessing, in his famous treatise *Laocoön*, tried to define the difference between poetry and the visual arts by showing how the same event was treated in a narrative poem and in a famous piece of sculpture, he defined the visual arts as happening in space without extension in time, whereas the narrative poem moved in time alone, without any spatial extension.

Drama, 'mimetic action unfolding itself in the present, and the presence, before the very eyes, of an audience, re-enacting fictional or real past events' is unique in that it combines the characteristics of narrative poetry and of the visual arts: it has both a spatial and a time dimension. It is a narrative made visible, a picture given the power to move in time.

The verbal portion of the dramatic event, insofar as it is present, proceeds, like a text a reader takes from the printed page, through time in a linear fashion, one word following another. But at the same time and intersecting with this linear axis the spectators of a dramatic performance are always confronted with a multidimensional spatial *image*, which is, at any given moment, presenting them with a multitude of items of information which are perceived simultaneously. The spectator, if he or she wants to become wholly conscious, or give a description of what he or she has instantly registered with his or her senses, then has to break that total image down into the separate items of information that have been present, and convert the multidimensional instant impression into a linear sequence of separate ingredients.

To illustrate this let us look at a simple example from outside the dramatic performance: if you are reading a weather report in a newspaper which says: 'rain is forecast for tomorrow' you get one piece of information and nothing else. If you hear the same weather report on the radio, you will, in addition, be made aware of the voice quality, male, female, deep or high-pitched, of the announcer, and of his mode of delivery: the announcer may sound cheerful or depressed about this piece of information.

But if you are getting this same report on television from an announcer or weatherman or weather-woman you will not only get all that additional information that radio conveys, but, apart from the fact that there will be rain tomorrow you will also be made aware of the fact that the (male) announcer is wearing a blue tie today; you are also made aware that today he looks tired (perhaps he has a hangover?). You also may get the information that a button is missing on his jacket. Or that the studio has green wallpaper – and so on and so on. There may be dozens, even hundreds of pieces of information all becoming available at the same instant in that image. What I have been doing, because you are reading this in print, is to break the image, or at least some of it, down into linear form and list some of the 'bits' of information it contains one after the other. And, of course, there are many, many more that are contained in the image the viewer has instantaneously perceived which could be listed.

In a dramatic performance you are getting audio-visual images of that type at every second and in each second the image on the stage or screen contains an enormous amount of items, 'bits', of information. Thus we can say that drama, on the stage and screen, communicates multidimensionally at any moment an almost inexhaustible amount of information and meaning. Some of this is taken in consciously by the spectator, other items of information are perceived subliminally, and will influence his or her subconscious reaction to the scene, others may remain quite unnoticed, and hence ineffective.

And for each member of the audience this impact of the image, at any given moment, will be different, simply because different people notice different things in a different sequence. Indeed, the writer, the director, the designer, the actors and all the other artists working on producing the image are doing their best to concentrate the audience's attention, at any given moment, on those elements in the scene that are most important. This is done by the grouping of the characters – Juliet high up on her balcony, spotlit so that everyone should have his attention focused on her. But even if the performance succeeds in drawing the spectators' attention to the desired spot at this time, the fact remains that the visual image projected at any given split-second in time to the audience will contain a multiplicity of different signs, items bearing bits of information and meaning, (what semioticians call 'signifiers'). Each of these signs contributes to the 'meaning' of the performance.

2

The performance space – whether it is the stage of the live theatre or the cinema and television screen – has a vital and truly fundamental aspect: by its very existence *it generates meaning*. It transforms the most ordinary and everyday trivia of existence into carriers of significance. Hang an empty picture frame on the wall – and suddenly the texture of the wall, the little smudges or spots on it become significant, they turn into an abstract painting of sorts. The frame makes anything within it significant. The stage, the cinema screen, the television tube are such frames.

When Marcel Duchamp put a urinal onto a pedestal and exhibited it in an art gallery, he made use of this magical quality of the stage. Anything that is perceived on a stage – or screen – by that very fact proclaims itself as being on exhibition, being pregnant with significance: one does not look at a urinal as a significant form when it is in everyday use. Being put onto a pedestal makes it visible as a perhaps beautiful, perhaps ugly, but certainly *significant* formal pattern that commands attention. Anyone who has ever had the experience of stepping onto a stage, even if only in an empty theatre, where he is being shown round, experiences that strange feeling that suddenly every move he or she makes becomes significant.

In the same way that a urinal put on a pedestal, or a person casually stepping onto a stage, immediately becomes transformed into something more significant, something on display, drama in performance is human life put onto a pedestal to be exhibited, looked at, examined and contemplated. And every detail of what is exhibited during the course of a dramatic performance, on stage or screen, becomes a sign, a 'signifier', one of the multifarious basic ingredients from which, in the mind of each individual spectator, the basic information about what is happening in the drama is perceived and established. And out of these basic facts the higher levels of its 'meaning' must ultimately emerge.

3

The image presented by a dramatic performance, whether in the theatre, cinema or on television is always three-dimensional, even though the cinema and television screens are flat. There is always the dimension of depth also present through the operation of perspective. But in these mechanically reproduced media the audience is in a space strictly separated from that in which the action of the drama is taking place. Here the frame of the screen is a window into a wholly separate space and the separation between the audience and the performers has become total – here they really are hermetically sealed from each other.

In the theatre the situation is different and often more complex: the audience and the stage are there in 'reality' always in a contiguous space, but in the 'fiction' of the play the stage also indicates a fictional space – that might either be of the same dimensions as it actually measures, or might represent spaces much larger or smaller than the one they occupy in 'reality'.

Moreover, in the theatre the performance *may* be based on the assumption that the characters on the stage are aware of the audience, if, for example, the actors directly address the audience, hence that a continuity of space is pre-supposed to exist between them; or, on the other hand, the characters on the stage may be supposed to be unaware that the space occupied by the audience is there at all.

The space in which the action proceeds in the cinema and television is – being photographs of 'real space' – always co-extensive with the scenes, landscapes or people it shows and it is freely extendable: the frame of the screen is an opening into which the spectator can be drawn at the behest of the director and cameraman to roam about in as far as is required.

In the theatre the stage, the platform on which the action proceeds, whether framed or not, has to serve for a multiplicity of possible spaces. It can present venues which share its 'real' dimensions or spaces infinitely larger than itself. Spaces that may, in 'reality', be miles apart may, on the stage be supposed to be simultaneously present, or to succeed each other within seconds, as the Aristotelian rules of unity of space are now being largely ignored by writers and directors.

4

Similarly, dramatic time also has been freed from any constraints: it can be compressed or expanded, speeded up or slowed down and can even – up to a point and within limits – overcome the irreversibility of the time-dimension; whereas 'real time' is unidirectional and once past can never recur, the time sequence of a play or film can be repeated.

Admittedly: once a dramatic performance has started it is compelled, relentlessly, to follow its prescribed path through time to its preordained end. Yet it is capable of being re-started again for another performance. In the case of the mechanically reproducible forms of drama – cinema and videotaped television drama – this quality of a sequence of moments permanently fixed in a certain order and infinitely repeatable becomes particularly clear, yet live drama has much of the same characteristics.

Within that repeatable time sequence itself, however, time may be represented in different ways:

The duration of the events on the stage or screen may be of the same length as it would be in reality, they would thus be happening in 'natural' time.

Or dramatic time may be foreshortened – so that events in the dramatic sequence are shown to be happening more swiftly than they would unfold in nature – within a continuous sequence that lasts, say ten minutes, events might be represented that would in reality take, say, two hours. Analogously events might be slowed down (this happens in the cinema when, for example, a violent event, a fight, a killing, might be shown in 'slow motion'; or, indeed on the stage, when for example time is slowed in a dream sequence).

Or, again, a series of events might be presented – either in their 'natural' duration, or foreshortened – but separated by gaps of days, months, even years.

Moreover, the time-scheme of a dramatic performance may violate the relentless, irreversible forward motion of time: events may be shown out of the chronological sequence which they, even in a fictional universe, would naturally follow; in drama, as in the novel, there can be flashbacks and flash-forwards, or the events may be shown in reverse order, as in Harold Pinter's *Betrayal* (as a stage play and a film), which starts by showing us lovers at the end of an affair and pursues its course back to its beginnings. Or the same time-span may be repeated again and again from different perspectives, as in Alan Ayckbourn's trilogy *The Norman Conquests* or the great Japanese film *Rashomon*. Time, in the fictional universe of drama, is highly malleable. That these matters of dramatic space and time are fundamental emerges from the fact that already Aristotle, in his *Poetics*, devoted special attention to this point: considerations of the treatment of space and time have always played an immense part in the different theories, rules and aesthetics of drama.

Dramatic time and space are the axes along which the multifarious sign systems of drama unfold themselves to its audiences.

IV

The Signs of Drama: Icon, Index, Symbol

I

Present-day semiotics, as first outlined by Peirce and developed and codified by contemporary semioticians like Roland Barthes, Umberto Eco, Erika Fischer-Lichte, Patrice Pavis, distinguishes three basic types of signs.

The simplest type of sign is the one that is instantly recognisable because it represents what it signifies by a direct image of that object, hence it is named by the Greek work for 'Picture' – *Icon*.

The 'pictures' can be realistic and photographic or highly stylised: the little bathtubs, wineglasses and beds in travel guides, the schematised figures in skirts or trousers on lavatory doors, all painted or photographic portraits of personalities that tell us what they looked like: they are all very obvious iconic signs. Iconic signs are, of course, very widespread – the entire artforms of representational painting, sculpture and photography can be regarded as systems of iconic signs. But not all icons are visual. The sound of a car horn in a play is an icon of the sound of a car horn.

All dramatic performance is basically iconic: every moment of dramatic action is a direct visual and aural sign of a fictional or otherwise reproduced reality. All other types of signs that are present in a dramatic performance operate within that basic iconic mimesis. The words of the dialogue, the gestures of the actors are signs of a different type, but they are present within the dramatic performance in the context of an iconic reproduction of their use in the 'reality' that is being 'imitated'.

The gestures we use in real life, and which the actors imitate, belong to another category of signs: signs which point to an object, like the arrows on street signs, or the movement I make when somebody asks me: 'Where is he?' and I point with my finger in the direction of the person concerned. These are called '*index*' signs, or also (when the derivation is from the Greek word for showing) 'deictic' signs. These signs derive their meaning from a relationship of contiguity to the object they depict. Personal pronouns, like 'you' or 'he' are deictic signs. We only know who is meant, if the word is accompanied by a gesture, or clearly alludes to a proper name previously mentioned. This type of sign obviously plays an important part in dramatic performance.

The third principal category of signs comprises those that have, unlike index signs and iconic signs, no immediately recognisable organic relationship to their 'signifieds'. This category of signs is called '*symbol*'. The meaning of symbolic signs derives entirely from convention – an agreement that, for example, the sounds D, O, G, dog, will be recognised as referring to a certain species of animal. Only those individuals who subscribe to this convention or agreement – in this case the speakers of English – will be able to understand the meaning of this arbitrary combination of sounds or letters. Most of our speech consists of such arbitrary symbolic signs. But there are many other symbolic signs in gestures, conventions of costume etc.

Index, icon, symbol – these, then, are the three main types of signs that semioticians distinguish.

Signs in the usual sense are tools deliberately employed to establish communication, tools through which one person, or a group of persons, intends to convey a meaning or message to another person. If someone has painted a picture of a landscape, he clearly intended to show his public what that landscape looked like; the pointing finger, the arrow on the road sign has been deliberately employed to point the recipients of the message in a certain direction; and all the symbolic signs are based on deliberate agreements between their users.

But there are also instances of 'meaning' being apprehended by an individual, even when there was and is no-one who intended to convey a message or meaning: events or phenomena that are interpreted to mean something without any deliberate intention of communication being involved. The sight of falling leaves in autumn, may be interpreted by me as being a sign that winter is about to come, or even as an intimation of the evanescence of youth or life; or if someone I am talking to suddenly blushes, I may take it as a sign that he is embarrassed, something which he does not intend to be made visible to me at all. Every event, any object whatever in the world can thus become a sign to an individual who perceives it. We speak of the Book of Nature that we can all read.

These omnipresent signs that have no conscious originator, but are liable to be perceived as having meaning by those who 'read' them, are what Umberto Eco in his *Theory of Semiotics* calls 'natural signs' (smoke rising can be read as a sign that there is a fire) and 'non-intentional signs' (spontaneous, involuntary human acts or gestures that 'give away' hidden emotions and can be read by an observer).[1] Not being intentional signs and thus not capable of being analysed as a 'language' or 'system' most conventional semiotics regard this category of 'involuntary' signs as outside their proper field.

In drama this category of 'natural' signs that, in the real world, exist without anyone deliberately producing them or intending to convey a message, assumes a special importance: dimming lights on the stage, a shot of the sinking sun on the screen, are deliberately used by the director to tell the audience that night is about to fall. The mimetic representation of a darkening sky has become an iconic sign of evening. Thus, in dramatic performance, what are 'natural' signs without a con-

[1] Eco, op. cit. p. 16/17

scious originator of their message become deliberately produced 'icons'. Yet these icons, in turn, may assume 'symbolic' functions: the darkening sky on the stage may be used by the director as a symbolic sign for the ending of a love affair, or death.

And the art of acting might be described as largely concerned with the deliberate, intentional, 'iconic' use of 'non-intentional', 'involuntary' signs or 'symptoms'. An actor who deliberately blushes on the stage produces an image – an iconic sign – of a person willy-nilly displaying such an 'involuntary' symptom of embarrassment. Indeed, it is part of the craft of acting, to be able to blush, laugh or cry at will.

The fascinatingly paradoxical, complicating factor here, however, is that while actors may produce these signs intentionally by simulating such states as sudden outbursts of crying, growing pale from fear, etc., it also often happens that the actors themselves exhibit these signs not by conscious intention, but involuntarily, spontaneously merely by using their imagination to produce the states of mind concerned, so that they themselves will simply start to blush or tremble or cry without any deliberate effort on their part to exhibit these particular symptoms.

What in the real world are 'non-intentional' signs, in dramatic performance, become deliberate 'iconic' representations of fear, embarrassment, etc. Yet the fact remains that, because here 'real' objects, and above all 'real' human beings are used as signs, an element of 'involuntary' semiosis will inevitably be involved in any dramatic performance: partly because the actors themselves may not be in total control of the expressions, gestures, etc. they exhibit, partly because material objects on the stage or screen may contain signifiers that the originators of the performance (the designer, the director) did not intend to be perceived. An actor may be 'mis-cast' and thus his appearance may suggest aspects that conflict with the author's or director's intentions: he or she may not be handsome or young enough. Or a character, say, in a historical play or film may be wearing a type of shoe which, to a member of the audience who is an expert in such matters, indicates the wrong historical period. Or the characters in a historical play or film may – as is only too often the case – use language that is obviously out of period for those who have sensitivity to the nuances of language. And we all know the example of the cat that strays accidentally onto the stage . . .

This penumbra of uncertainty and inexactness that springs from the presence of involuntary and unintentional signs, highlights the very special situation of dramatic performance as an object for semiotics. Most iconic signs used in other fields are both deliberately produced and capable of being simply understood, interpreted (or as the jargon puts it: 'decoded') by those for whom they have been intended. A painting of a horse will be read by all and sundry as representing a horse. Even an abstract painting will be perceived as a deliberately ambiguous image, or as a statement about pure form and colour. Iconic signs, moreover, can be very simplified representations of the objects they signify, and therefore concentrate on a single meaning. The lady on the powder-room door is, in fact, very unlike a real lady; a highly abstract – and conventional – symbol which tells us, unambiguously, no more than that this figure has a skirt while the one opposite has trousers. There are those who argue that we recognise these images because we have *learned* to read them, that they themselves are conventional, almost like hieroglyphs or Chinese ideograms – which indeed, mark the borderline between the iconic and the symbolic type of sign.

Yet in drama, as far as the human characters are concerned, there is no abstraction: there a lady appears and she is a completely concrete lady who is being shown to us as the icon – the iconic sign – for a fictional lady. The director who shows us an actress portraying Juliet or Ophelia is telling us: this is what Juliet or Ophelia looked like. The icon here at least aims at suggesting a complete identity in looks between the 'signifier' (the actress) and the 'signified' (the fictional character).

The same is true of many of the objects we see on the stage, even more so of the world depicted in the photographic reality of filmed or televised drama.

Yet there is a very decisive distinction to be made between the inevitable concreteness of the human individual and the tendency of many of the iconic signs used in drama towards increasing abstraction: highly schematised objects can approach the status of ideograms, as when a mere frame suggests a door on the stage, or three soldiers an army, or the mere gesture of drinking replaces a glass of water; or in the cinema a shot of Big Ben or the Manhattan skyline is used as shorthand for a shift of the action to London or New York.

The human figure and its gestures are the most powerful source of suggestion on the stage: to the point when, in certain single character plays, one actor talking to the void may suggest the presence of a second, non-existent, interlocutor.

2

The types of sign we have discussed – icon; index; symbol; as well as the 'involuntary' (natural or non-intentional) iconic signs without a deliberate originator – combine, in dramatic performance, in a multitude of different sign systems, or 'languages', each with its own 'grammar' and 'syntax' (although the analogy with verbal languages must always be treated with caution, as each sign system has its own limitations).

For example: there is a 'language' of gestures. Some of our gestures are 'deictic' – pointing fingers, frightened looks; others are 'iconic' – we all instantly recognise the meaning of an embrace, an angry blow etc.; others again are 'symbolic': in oriental theatre the slightest movement of a finger may have a definite meaning which, by age-old convention, the spectators have learned to interpret and understand; in Western drama at certain periods there were also such formalised symbolic gestures: in the melodrama of the nineteenth century, for example, turning the face away and lowering the head had become a symbol of grief – here an iconic representation of what happens when someone is suddenly struck by grief had been formalised, ritualised and made into a conventional symbolic gesture. Many such sign systems, many more than in any other art form, are simultaneously at work in dramatic performance.

Yet we may ask: what is the purpose, what are the benefits to spectators, critics, performers, of analysing the typology of signs and sign systems; why should we want to know what types of signs, what sign systems, are present in a given production and how they interact, combine and contradict each other dialectically?

The simplest answer, it seems to me, is that this is the most practical, down-to-earth approach to the act of communication that every dramatic performance is intended to establish: by analysing what signs and sign systems, in what interaction, are present and at least potentially operating upon the sensibilities of the recipients of the communication – the audience – we should arrive at the most concrete, factual basis for gaining a clear conception of what actually takes place in an artistic event like a play or film, far less airy-fairy and abstract than analyses of the psychology of characters or philosophical implications. These, the psychologies and philosophies, are always implied and well worth enlarging upon, but, surely only after the basic bedrock of what actually took place on stage or screen has been established.

As for those responsible for originating a dramatic performance, clearly, a knowledge of what each gesture, each look, each detail of set-design, facial make-up and all the many different, 'meaning-producing' elements of a performance can and should signify and how they interact and combine, must be of decisive importance. That each contributor to the production (director, designer, actors, lighting designer and musician) should be an expert in his own field, whether his knowledge is theoretical or merely practical-intuitive, is obvious. But a methodology for a clear analysis of what actually is going on in a performance, and of how the individual elements operate from which the total 'meaning' of the performance will emerge, should clearly be of value.

And to know how a given sign operates and what kind of sign it is, how it fits into the ultimate over-all effect that is intended must certainly be useful: when the stage darkens at a certain point, will the spectators be inclined to interpret that as an 'iconic' image of the daylight fading in the evening, or will it be seen as a 'symbolic' sign that the situation of the leading character is becoming gloomier, or perhaps both at the same time: the descent of night becoming a symbol of tragedy or misfortune. A knowledge of the 'grammar' and 'syntax' of the interaction of the different signs and sign systems should thus help the director to attain a higher degree of certainty that he will actually convey the meaning he intended, at least to the majority of the audience.

Similarly a clear awareness of how a performance works, and how and why it perhaps fails to work, based on an analysis of all the means that were brought into play by the originators of the performance, should be of considerable help in the critical discussion of a dramatic performance. A semiotic approach should be able to avoid the mere impressionism that besets much dramatic criticism both by daily reviewers and by academics.

As to the spectator: it could be argued that an audience member should merely sit back and let the performance do its work. This view is widespread, but, surely, it is based on a somewhat naive idea of what art is and how it creates its effects. All art, and the art of drama in particular, is largely based on conventions that must be shared between the artist and his audience and must therefore be an acquired skill that, ultimately, must be learned. Much of this learning process occurs almost spontaneously simply through steady and prolonged exposure to the ruling conventions. But true sophistication, the ability to derive the fullest enjoyment, enlightenment and spiritual experience from art does depend on a form of expertise. Connoisseurship of any kind, of wines, paintings, and naturally also of dramatic performance, must involve a good deal of skill and sophistication – of learned experience.

The spectator of a football match or a cricket or baseball game derives maximum excitement and enjoyment only if he or she is familiar with the rules by which those games are played, and the finer points of strategy, tactics and technique. To derive the maximum pleasure and perhaps some of the higher insights that drama can give, a knowledge of the methods, conventions and finer points of theatrical performance, or the camera's movements and editing in the cinema and television, in short, a high degree of sophistication, must similarly be useful.

While it may be an over-ambitious project to reduce the semiotics of dramatic performance to an 'exact science' (capable of producing an exact record of the signifiers at work at any given moment of a performance and assigning them their exact 'meaning') a semiotic approach to dramatic performance should, nevertheless, prove a useful and, above all, practical approach, a worth-while methodology, towards establishing an understanding of how the groundwork, the prime constituents of a dramatic performance, its *basic meaning* – what Brecht calls 'the fable' – emerges and crystallizes from the interaction and combination of all the different sign-systems present and operating throughout its course.

V

The Signs of Drama: The Frame

In his influential book *Littérature et Spectacle*[1] Tadeusz Kowzan listed thirteen sign systems involved in stage presentation (all of which should be equally applicable to the other visual dramatic media): 1) words, 2) delivery of the text, 3) facial expression, 4) gesture, 5) the movement of the actors in the dramatic space, 6) make-up, 7) hair-do, 8) costume, 9) properties, 10) sets, 11) lighting, 12) music, 13) sound effects.[2]

Kowzan remarks that the first two of these 'sign systems' refer to the text, the next three (3 to 5) to the expressive use of the actor's body, the next three (6 to 8) to the outward appearance of the actor, numbers 9 to 11 to the visuals of the stage and the last two to sound – five groups of sign systems in all, of which the first three (1 to 8) directly concern the actor.[3]

This list contains some puzzling omissions as well as inclusions, even if only as an enumeration of the primary producers of meaning common to all drama. Why, to cite but one example, should the hair-do of the actors be a separate system and not be regarded as merely one aspect of make-up? Is a moustache pasted to an actor's upper lip part of his hair-do, or of his make-up? The dividing lines between most of the sign systems used in drama are fluid, but in this case there seems little point

[1] Tadeusz Kowzan, *Littérature et Spectacle*, The Hague and Paris: Mouton, 1975.
[2] Kowzan, p. 182 ff.
[3] ibid. p. 205.

in drawing such lines at all. On the other hand Kowzan's list contains some surprising omissions.

In drawing up an alternative table of primary sign systems we must start with one cluster of sign systems Kowzan overlooked:

Framing and preparatory indicators

To function as a sign the sign must above all be recognised as a sign, marked as a sign. The frame of a picture, the sign-post on which the street sign is exhibited, the act of making eye-contact with the person to whom a speech act is addressed, are the basis of all communication. In the case of drama the shape of the theatrical space, the 'ambiance', the 'atmosphere' of the theatre or cinema, or, indeed in the case of television, the absence of these atmospheric factors, play a vital part in the overall effect and meaning of the dramatic event for the spectator.

There is a vast difference between the sense of occasion (and hence the importance of the significance of what is presented) which is created by a sumptuous theatre filled with people in evening-dress on the one hand and, on the other, the informality of a cinema, filled with the smell of pop-corn, or indeed the absence of such a sense of occasion, the casualness with which the same film is received at home on a small screen surrounded by the clutter of the viewer's accustomed surroundings.

Whether drama is watched in the various types of theatrical architecture, from the proscenium arch to 'theatre in the round', on different types of cinema screen (small, wide, or cinerama) or television receivers, must considerably influence its impact. No analysis of the genesis of meaning can neglect this basic aspect.

It is the stage or screen itself which acts as the primary generator of meaning. However trivial an object or an event may appear in the 'real world', as soon as it is perceived on a stage or a cinema or television screen, it is immediately raised to the level of a sign. Yet the stage or screen itself, and the building or setting in which they are situated, exert a powerful influence on the expectations of the audience and the way they will read the signs presented to them by the performance. A mystery play performed in a church will have a different meaning from that which would emerge were the same performance presented in a cabaret (when some spectators might take it for parody); the same film will have different impacts on a large screen in a luxurious cinema, in a flea-pit and on a small television set.

Nor must we forget the many multifarious additional framing devices that usually tend to be overlooked, because they are so familiar as to have become as invisible as the postman in Chesterton's Father Brown story. These include, above all, the **title and the generic description of the piece** – 'a comedy in three acts', 'a Western' which set the mood and the 'level of expectation' – the 'Erwartungshorizont' of German 'Rezeptionsaesthetik' (aesthetics of audience response). Some of these initial pointers towards the mood in which the performance is to be viewed will be perceived by the playgoer in **lights above the entrance** (with the names of the stars, themselves highly effective arousers of expectation) or in the **programme brochure** he or she is handed when taking his or her seat; but even before that, his expectations may have been set by **pre-publicity** in the newspapers, reports on the play by friends who have seen it earlier, and, probably most influential of all, by the reviews of it he may have read; in the cinema they include all those, plus the publicity posters and trailers, as well as the opening title sequence. In television pre-title sequences containing 'appetizers' from the drama to follow, as well as the elaborate title sequences themselves are of decisive importance in a medium where the technique by which individual items gain attention amid the unending flow of programmes and commercials plays a decisive role not only in setting the receptive mood of the spectators but in actually inducing them to settle on watching the show.

The level at which expectations are pitched at the outset has an often crucial influence on the way the 'meaning' of individual signifiers as well as the total meaning of the performance is understood. These preliminary, or framing, devices belong to a higher order of sign than any individual signifiers, as they set the initial mood, the level at which all other signs are to be 'decoded'. They are comparable to the 'keys' of musical notation.

In periods in the history of drama, when newspaper advertising and reviewing, the neon-lit letters above the entrance, the programme brochure or the cinematic title sequence were unavailable, this all-important semiotic function was performed by 'prologues' that set the scene and the level of expectation; as well as 'epilogues' that completed the frame and added some retrospective elucidation which undoubtedly affected the ultimate residue of the play's 'message' in the recollection of the audience.

Kowzan starts his list of the sign systems of theatre with the 'words': the text that is spoken. This seems to be a relic of the view that the primary factor in drama is the text. Yet there is drama without words: mime, the silent cinema, ballet. It may thus be more logical to start the list of the sign systems used within the performance with the pivot around which all drama in performance revolves: **the actor**.

VI

The Signs of Drama: The Actor

I

The actor is the iconic sign *par excellence*: a real human being who has become a sign for a human being.

In a brilliant and provocative essay on 'The Semiotics of Theatrical Performance'[1] in which he sketches out some basic considerations of the problems of such a branch of knowledge, before gracefully neglecting to come to grips with it, Umberto Eco cites C. S. Peirce's speculations about a case in which a human being becomes a sign: a drunkard on a platform outside a Salvation Army meeting house, exposed to illustrate the ravages of drink.

Eco points out that a sign, according to Peirce's definition, is 'something that stands for somebody or something else in some respect or capacity'. The drunken man thus is a sign not for himself but for the general category of 'drunks'. The sign thus might stand for sentences like: 'there is a drunken man here' or 'once upon a time there was a drunken man' or 'there are many drunken men in the world'. The drunken man has been chosen to act as a sign because some features about him (by no means all his characteristics or qualities, but only some, essential for the purpose of 'ostension' [semiotic jargon for 'showing']) make him 'typical' – in other words he is not displayed as himself but as a specimen of a whole class of human beings. In this respect, Eco argues, the choice of this particular drunk by the Salvation

[1] Umberto Eco, 'Semiotics of Theatrical Performance' in *The Drama Review*, vol. 21 No 1 (T 73), March 1977).

Army is analogous to the choice of the right word in formulating a sentence. Except that a word is a sign without physical resemblance or relationship to its referent, whereas

> 'the drunk is a sign, but he is a sign that pretends not to be such. The drunkard is playing a double game: in order to be accepted as a sign, he has to be recognized as a real spatio-temporal event, a real human body. In theatre there is a 'square semiosis'. With words, a phonic object stands for other objects made with different stuff. In the mise-en-scène an object, first recognized as a real object, is then assumed as a sign in order to refer back to another object (or to a class of objects) whose constitutive stuff is the same as that of the representing object'[2]

Eco's use of Peirce's paradigm is most stimulating and raises a number of important issues: it, incidentally, draws attention to the importance of 'framing' – not only does the platform on which he stands transform the ordinary drunk into a sign, but the fact that it is a Salvation Army platform, instantly recognisable as such, makes the drunk, the victim of alcoholism, to stand 'ironically for his contrary; he celebrates the advantages of temperance'.

But as an analogy for dramatic performance, Eco's example is incomplete and misses some of the essential points. For in a true dramatic context the drunkard would not be a real drunkard but an actor deliberately simulating the characteristics (the red nose, the bleary eyes etc.) of the drunkard and the audience would be aware of his *skill* in doing so. Apart from recognising the drunkard as a member of a class of human beings and perhaps understanding the message he represents as a warning against alcohol, they will also appreciate and applaud his 'artistry' in producing that effect (or boo him for failing to do so). Moreover, in a dramatic performance the drunkard would, most likely, not merely be an anonymous presence. He would, almost certainly, be playing an individualised fictitious charac-

[2] loc. cit. p. 111.

ter and thus function as a sign for a *fictional individual* as well as a member of a class of individuals. So that the semiotic role of the actor in a dramatic event is far more complex than Eco's paradigm suggests.

An actor appearing on the stage or screen is, in the first place, himself, the 'real' person that he is with his physical characteristics, his voice and temperament; he is, secondly, himself, transformed, disguised, by costume, make-up, an assumed voice, a mental attitude derived from the study of and empathy with the fictional character he is playing: this is the 'stage-figure' as the Prague school has dubbed him, the physical simulacrum of the character; but, thirdly, and most importantly there is the 'fiction' itself, for which he stands, and which ultimately will emerge in the mind of the individual spectator watching the play or film. That spectator, for example, may well notice that the actress – and the stage figure – that represents Juliet is not outstandingly beautiful or attractive; yet in his imagination he will, having understood that she is *supposed* to be outstandingly beautiful, complete the picture, and 'read' the action as though he was seeing an outstandingly beautiful girl. And that fictional figure, in turn, may, like Eco's drunken man, also stand for a whole category or class of individuals, may assume general human meaning.

This extremely complex state of affairs produces its own, highly suggestive and artistically fascinating ambiguities and inner tensions:

An actor playing Hamlet is a sign for the fictional character of Hamlet with all that fictional person's complex individuality. He may also become in the eyes of some members of the audience a representative of a class of individuals (princes, intellectuals who think too much, sons in love with their mothers, the human predicament itself and a multitude of others), but also, unlike the drunk in Peirce's example cited by Eco, he will retain much of his real personality as the actor he is known to be. The semiosis will here not merely be, as Eco posits it for the drunk, 'squared', it will be 'cubed', for the man here stands for a sign that stands for a man who, in turn, is recognised and valued as the original man that he is. It is the tension between the real actor on the one hand, and the fictional character for whom he functions as an iconic sign on the other, that creates one of the main attractions of drama in performance. The audience never forgets that the iconic function of the actor is playful pretence. The suspension of disbelief in the theatre, the cinema or in front of the television screen does not go so far that the sign is taken for the reality. Indeed, most theories of drama, from the ancient Greeks to Brecht, build on that particular tension. A far greater proportion of audiences go to the theatre or cinema or watch television to see particular actors rather than the fictional characters they signify. The economics of the theatre, cinema and television, with their emphasis on the drawing power of the 'star', are built on that fact.

The actor thus is the essential ingredient around which all drama revolves. There can be, and has been, drama without writers, designers, directors – there can never be drama without actors. Even the marionettes of the puppet or shadow theatre, the moving drawings or model figures of animated film, are actors, iconic signs that stand for people or humanised animals and they have, of course, also the voices of human actors.

The actor, as he stands on the stage, or appears on the screen, moreover is more than a mere sign for a fictional character as conceived by the imagination of a writer. His *personality* itself, the indefinable uniqueness of an individual human being, the personal magnetism emanating from him or her, adds additional signifiers to those provided by the inventor of the fiction. The words spoken by Gielgud as Hamlet carry a slightly different meaning from those spoken by Olivier or Guinness in the same role, not only because each of these performers gives them a different reading through the different timbre of his voice, different stresses and timing, but simply by being spoken by a different human being.

This emphasises the profoundly *erotic* nature of drama. The sheer magnetism of human personality is itself a powerful generator of 'meaning'. When a beautiful woman in the role of, say, Juliet steps onto the stage, her appearance signifies: 'This fictional girl was as beautiful as this; Juliet looked like this!' The whole impact, the whole 'meaning' of the play will turn around that basic fact.

It is sometimes argued that this erotic element only operates, or operates more strongly, in the 'live' theatre and is one of the factors more or less absent in the cinema or on television, because it is only the physical presence of the actor or actress that can generate that 'erotic' impact. This view, surely, is constantly disproved by the impact star performers, from Greta Garbo to Marilyn Monroe, from Clark Gable to Robert Redford, have had in the cinema, as well as the reliance of television on similar star personalities. What the mechanically reproduced media lack in physical presence, they more than make up by their ability to bring the viewer into far greater proximity to the performer, by close-ups that create an illusion of physical proximity to the attractive person far greater than the theatre could ever hope to achieve, even for the spectators in the best seats.

2

The basically erotic nature of the attraction of actors accounts for the immense importance of **casting** in dramatic performance. 'Casting' is one of the most basic semiotic systems that generate its meaning. And it is not merely the attractiveness or magnetism of individual performers that has its semiotic weight, but the *interaction* between several of them. The balance of personalities in a dramatic performance itself is one of the principal determinants of its ultimate 'meaning', one of the basic artistic decisions the director must make that will underlie his interpretation of the fiction and determine its impact and ultimate significance.

In addition to the basic meaning-generating quality of his own personality and erotic magnetism the actor has at his disposal an array of sign systems, which could be grouped as comprising, on the one hand, those derived from the expressive techniques based on the use of his or her body: use of the voice in modulating the text, facial expression, gesture ('kinesics'), and grouping or movement in space ('proxemics') and, on the other hand, those the actor *carries* on his body: make-up and costume.

These systems, of course, constantly inter-act: an actor's costume may well greatly influence his gestures and movement (heavy sleeves may enlarge his gestures, a narrow skirt may influence an actress's walk); make-up obviously influences facial expression, etc.

What must also always be kept in mind in analysing the production of meaning in acting is a basic paradox: the actor himself is an icon – a human being acting as a sign for a human being. But a number of the sign systems he uses may themselves be either iconic, deictic or symbolic, or all three at the same time. Thus a white beard is an *iconic* sign of old age, but may also be intended as a *symbolic* indication of wisdom. A conspicuous wig may be an *icon* of a conceited character, but, at the same time may function as a *deictic* sign to draw the audience's attention to the character (to make him, for example, stand out in a group).

This is true of those sign systems that the actor employs intentionally and with deliberation. In addition, acting raises, in a particularly clear form, as Umberto Eco also stresses, the problem of the so-called 'non-intentional' sign. If someone blushes that is a sign that he is embarrassed, even though he wants to hide the fact. An actor, if he is skilled, should be a master of producing such seemingly involuntary signs, at will, and with deliberation. They are icons of the meaning he wants to express; they contain information that he wants to purvey. But it may well also happen, particularly when the actor has been trained in techniques emphasising empathy with the character's state of mind, that that state of mind spontaneously finds expression in the form of natural, involuntary signs, such as blushing, without the actor deliberately employing a technique to create a blush on his face. And, indeed, certain schools of acting concentrate on the actor 'living' his role in his imagination with such intensity that these signs will appear spontaneously and without his own conscious intervention. If the emotion of the character is truly felt, the expression of it will spontaneously manifest itself to the audience. (Diderot's dialogue *Paradoxe sur le comédien* was one of the first to highlight the conflict between an 'emotive' and a 'deliberate' school of acting.)

Yet even an actor who has consciously planned every nuance of expression, may display unintended signifiers, which may introduce elements of meaning into a performance that he never planned and of which he remains unaware. For example: he may hesitate, when the character is to be fluent, fail to blush when he should do so, or blush when he is not to blush. Or he may simply be too old for his role (by having been 'miscast') and will thus convey – at least to some members of the audience – information that he is very far from wanting to provide. While some of these unintended elements may simply be due to incompetence or lack of artistic talent, it must always be remembered that every performance, however brilliant and competent its originators, is bound to carry an aura of such unintended overtones. The very fact that, in a 'run' of 'live' performances the actors will become aware that on certain evenings 'everything worked', an electrifying atmosphere was generated, while at others it did not 'come together', attests the presence of such unintended, unplannable, factors. In the cinema even the very best shot, selected from the many that were taken of a single scene, may well carry a number of such unintended factors as well. The same applies even more forcefully to television where the opportunities for 're-takes' are much fewer, owing to more compressed shooting schedules.

In analysing the process of acting it is useful to be aware of the nature and function of the interplay of the sign systems at the actor's command.

In the **vocal interpretation** of the text, for instance, there is the difference between a purely iconic – naturalistic or realistic – delivery which aims at as accurate a reproduction of natural speech as possible on the one hand, and the more 'declamatory' styles in which the raising or lowering of the pitch, the quickening or slowing of the tempo, the use of 'vibrato', a deep voice for serious and a light voice for playful subject-matter, have fixed symbolic meanings.

The same is true of **facial expression** where the spectrum also extends from the reproduction of natural expression (from the simulated 'non-intentional' sign as an icon of the emotion) at one end, to, at the other, the highly formalised artistry of, for example, oriental styles of theatre, where the raising of an eye-brow, the twitching of the corners of the mouth have definite conventional symbolic meanings.

Such symbolic elements are even more evident in the sphere of **gesture** and **movement** not only in such styles as Japanese Noh and Kabuki, Chinese classical opera or Indian Kathakali, but also in Western dramatic styles of a more formal nature, as embodied, to cite but one famous example, in Goethe's rules for his actors in eighteenth-century Weimar, which precisely prescribed posture and position on stage for the actors according to their characters' 'rank' in society. For example:

> Nor should the actors play to each other as if no third person were present. This would be a case of misunderstood naturalness. They should never act in profile nor turn their backs to the spectators.
>
> ... It is an important point that when two are acting together, the speaker should always move upstage, while the one who has stopped speaking should move slightly downstage.

> ... The person of higher social scale (women, elders, noblemen) always occupies the right side.... Whoever stands at the right should insist on his prerogative and not allow himself to be driven towards the wings ...[3]

Make-up and costume also employ a considerable element of symbolic signifiers, even in otherwise realistically iconic contexts – witness the convention of the black costume for the villain in the classical Western. Make-up and hairstyle tend to be more highly charged with symbolic signifiers in oriental drama, while they tend towards iconic realism in the West. But even here there is often a symbolic subtext beneath the realistic surface.

3

The manner in which an actor speaks the words he is given is of course of crucial importance to the meaning of drama. The written form of a text is far from containing an unambiguous statement of its 'real' meaning. Indeed Jacques Derrida is undoubtedly right when he denies the possibility of a text containing one single ultimately correct ('metaphysical') meaning. The actor thus by necessity produces (sometimes via the director's promptings) what must ultimately be his own individual 'reading' of the text, which in turn, of course, becomes a new 'text' open to innumerable individual 'readings' of it by the audience.

Take any line from the written text of any play and try the experiment of stressing each word in turn. Even the simplest phrase subtly changes its meaning: GOOD Morning! means something slightly different from Good MORNING! by the change of stress alone. Add to this all the other variables: rising or falling cadence; asserting or questioning intonation; soft or loud, fast or slow, meek or imperious delivery; the insertion of a pause before, after or in the middle of the phrase.

[3] From Goethe, 'Rules for Actors' in A. M. Nagler, *A Source Book of Theatrical History*, N. Y.: Dover, 1952, p. 429/30.

It can be argued that the vocal line of sung forms of drama, particularly in recitativo, is an attempt to fix the vocal delivery of the words more rigidly and accurately than is possible in purely spoken dialogue. Certain directors who tend to treat the actor as an 'Übermarionette' (super-puppet) have also tried to hold their actors to a fixed pre-determined vocal line. Reinhardt sometimes marked the intonations in his 'Regiebuch' (his meticulously prepared plan for each production) with musical notation.

Yet, of course, the meaning of the words on the printed page of a text or screenplay, is not only determined by the vocal delivery alone. We must add all the other indicators from other sign systems – a glum or cheerful facial expression, a wide variety of gestures, a slow or fast movement towards or away from the character who is being addressed etc. – and it will be evident that even the simplest phrase can yield an enormous gamut of different meanings. If that is true of two trivial words, the possible permutations for the delivery of an entire text grow to an almost infinite number, greater than the possible moves in a game of chess. The manifold potential variations in stress and pitch of the words of a dramatic text thus add a powerful deictic element to their symbolic meaning as mere verbal language.

In the systems of facial expression and gesture deictic signs obviously also play an important part. A look or a pointing finger often contain essential information supplementing the text. '... I took by the throat the circumcised dog, and smote him – thus ...' (*Othello*, V, ii) is a very clear example of how the text demands the gesture which in turn alone gives its full meaning to the words. The word 'thus' compels the actor to make a gesture; it achieves its full meaning only when that gesture is carried out. This is a very clear instance of the way a well-written dramatic text can and should already contain and compel the actor's gestures. Brecht's term 'gestural language' points to the interdependence, and sometimes dialectical, contrapuntal relationship between the verbal and the facial or gestural sign systems in drama. This can be summed up in the principle that words should only be used when the potential of these non-verbal, visual sign systems has been exhausted. It is, for example, astonishing how much gestural content in the text, say, of Shakespeare's plays, emerges during rehearsal, when the deictic words like 'here', 'there', 'thus' only begin to reveal their full meaning from the physical situation obtaining at a given point in a given scene. And the same is true of all plays relying on a great deal of physical action – the *lazzi* of commedia dell'arte, the 'gags' of farce.

In the cinema and in television, where close-ups can bring the actor into intimate proximity with the spectator the amount of information and significance carried by these sign systems alone increases enormously and proportionately decreases the importance of the verbal element.

The audience's decoding and interpretation of facial expression and gesture is, by the very nature of those sign systems, far more instinctive and subliminal than that of the verbal or design elements. 'Body language' from the most spectacular posture down to the most minute flicker of the eyelids is among the most primitive of all communication media, one that human beings share with the higher animals; it evokes many almost totally instinctive, automatic responses. This is the sphere where the spectator's 'gut reaction' generates the most intense 'empathy' between the fictional character embodied in the actor and the spectator. Eyes opened wide in terror, arms threateningly raised to deliver a heavy blow, or, indeed, a woman meltingly sinking into a man's embrace are physically 'felt' by the concentrated spectator. And these emotions generate the appropriate physical response in the audience: faster pulse-rate, heavier breathing, tension in the pit of the stomach, even the physical symptoms of sexual arousal. Here emotion is almost telepathically transferred from the stage or screen to the audience. Hence, a dramatic medium, striving for the maximum of attention, like television, tends to resort to violence, precisely because of this direct physical impact of dramatic action: its compelling, involving, and almost wholly instinctive power.

This is also the area where voluntarily, and unconsciously, instinctively, produced signifiers are most intricately intermingled in the performance of the actors.

4

Movement within the dramatic space (as against the movement of the camera's point of view in cinema and television, and thus far more important on the stage) also contains elements of this deeply instinctive response. The distance between the characters, their movement towards or away from each other, their relative positions on the vertical plane – above or below each other, their standing, sitting down and getting up, are of paramount expressive significance, as are the angles at which they confront each other and the audience. An entrance from the diagonal has a very different impact from one at right angles to, or frontally towards, the auditorium.

Walking across the stage, standing still, increasing or diminishing the distance between two characters, the grouping of characters in significant patterns are all instances of the signifying power of the movement in space ('proxemics' in semiotic jargon) of the actors in drama.

Such movement has its obvious iconic function, but can also become a deictic signifier: a character who suddenly gets up, sits down or moves about the stage draws attention upon himself. But frequently movement in dramatic space also acquires symbolic meaning: when Brand in Ibsen's great play ascends the mountain his upward movement acquires a spiritual significance, while the pratfalls of the characters in Beckett's plays indicate their earthbound nature.

When in Pinter's *The Basement* a character sits down in a chair, that may indicate that he has taken possession of the room. But even in the most realistic drawing room comedy, getting up from a chair or sitting down again carries important psychological and dramatic significance.

Changes in the spatial distribution of the characters not only serve as a very necessary means of articulation of the flow of the action, as indicators when a beat or segment of the scene is over and a new one starts, they must also always be justifiable by the psychological situation of the characters and expressive of the dramatic situation at that point in the action.

John Gabriel Borkman ceaselessly walking up and down in his room like a caged animal, Winnie in Beckett's *Happy Days* stuck in a mound of earth and sinking ever deeper, Hamlet leaping into Ophelia's tomb, Don Juan being swallowed by the Mouth of Hell, the characters grouped in clusters of twos and threes on a wide stage in Chekhov's *Cherry Orchard* or Gorky's *Lower Depths* (with the hidden tensions among them made palpably visible) are examples of how such movement – or its momentary freezing into static patterns in space – can encapsulate essential aspects of the meaning of the dramas concerned in a single dynamic image.

From the earliest times elaborate stage-machinery has been used to produce surprising and spectacular effects of movement: the appearance from on high of the 'deus ex machina', the angels flying across the stage in Florentine mystery plays performed in churches, or Peter Pan flying in through the nursery window.

That 'pure' movement can, without a spoken text, powerfully generate 'meaning' is forcefully illustrated by those extreme cases of dramatic forms in which movement dominates – mime, dance and ballet – and this not only on the stage but also in the cinematic media: think of the dances and production numbers in the musical film (as exemplified by the work of Busby Berkeley, Bob Fosse and many others) or the immense expressiveness of ballet on television.

In the sphere of movement and spatial disposition instinctive responses, conventional and symbolic meanings also intermingle with purely iconic representation. The King sitting on his throne on a dais above his subjects realistically portrays the situation in the real throne-room as well as expressing a symbolic meaning, while his occupying the highest position also has a deictic aspect – he is made the focal point of the action.

In this case the iconic sign merely reproduces the symbolic sign system already obtaining in the 'real world', yet there are many cases of outwardly realistic 'arrangements' or 'groupings' that also carry a large amount of spatial symbolism of a generally conventional nature, or arising out of a specific dramatic situation: as when Hamlet stands apart from the courtiers surrounding the royal couple, or Romeo looks upward at Juliet on her balcony adoring her as a creature of a higher order of nature.

In the field of mime – the dramatic art form that assigns the main signifying function to movement – there is both an iconic and a symbolic approach: there are those artists who try to imitate and stylise natural movement – much of Marcel Marceau's work is of this nature – while other tendencies in Europe and the Far East have evolved elaborate and complex symbolic vocabularies of gestures, each of which has a definite meaning; the pantomimic theatre of the great French mime Debureau was of this nature, as is the system of Étienne Decroux, the great mime teacher of this century; and Indian Kathakali.

The same is true of **make-up** and **costume**: in some oriental types of drama there is an elaborate code prescribing the meaning of masks, make-up and garments. In Western drama hairstyles and beards and a wide variety of costumes simultaneously convey conventional – and hence symbolic – significance as well as communicating realistic – iconic – information, while, at the same time they also act as deictic indicators, pointing to the central character in a scene by a more sumptuous or more colourful costume, hair-do or make-up.

Conventional costumes connected with function and occupation indicate whether a character is upper-class or proletarian, parlour-maid, policeman, gangster, soldier or doctor (or, in earlier social contexts, shoemaker, carpenter or smith). The information conveyed by costume and make-up is often an essential element in the exposition of drama.

The spectator of drama must have something of the talents of that archetypal semiotician, Sherlock Holmes, who was able to discover the most copious and accurate information from the scars on the face and the minutest elements in the dress of any person he met. The tiniest details in the appearance of a character, the cut of his garments, the colour of his complexion, the specks of dirt on his clothes contain an enormous amount of information, and thus play an important part in the delineation of character on the stage, but even more so on the screen, where close-ups can draw attention to the smallest significant elements. In drama originating from wholly different cultures – Indian or Japanese films for example – Western audiences unfamiliar with their codes are often at a loss to understand the characters. Yet it must always be kept in mind that this decoding process is only partially conscious: many members of the audience will tend to react instinctively to the 'general impression' produced by the confluence of a multitude of subliminally perceived characteristics, from the cut of the garments to the mud on the character's shoes (as indeed we react to people we meet in 'real' life).

In addition to the numerous details in costume and make-up which combine to create the over-all, largely subliminal, *impression* the character generates, costume also contributes powerfully to the mood, the aura surrounding the fictional person by using the symbolic power of the colour scheme of his facial make-up, hair-do and clothing. To this symbolic function of make-up and costume must be added its deictic function: the more important characters are highlighted and attention is focused on them, by more spectacular or contrasting costume and make-up.

In addition, as already mentioned, make-up and costume can

play a part in reinforcing the effectiveness of the sign systems of facial expression, gesture and movement. Wigs, the cut of clothes, the style of footwear can increase or reduce an actor's (and his character's) height and girth, can compel him to make his gestures larger or smaller and affect the way he moves. And all these details carry significance on an iconic, symbolic and deictic level.

Costume and make-up were traditionally left to the actor himself. In more recent times they have increasingly been decided by the designers of dramatic productions. In this case, therefore, there is overlap between the spheres of the sign systems centred on the actor and those that are essentially the domain of the scene designer and other specialists in the visual aspects of dramatic performance such as the designers of costume, make-up and lighting.

VII

The Signs of Drama: Visuals and Design

I

The most basic sign system by which the designer contributes to the complex interaction of signifiers that generate information and meaning in a dramatic performance, even before he presents an iconic or symbolic 'picture', is that of the **infrastructure of 'spaces'** he creates. This decisively determines the pattern of the actors' movement. By laying the groundwork for the manner and speed of their motion the designer has a profound influence on the performance of the actors: how they enter and exit, ascend and descend stairs, approach and recede from the audience in highly meaningful directions (diagonal, full-face, profile) and thus express a multitude of moods and meanings.

The rise of the modern director is closely connected with the recognition of the potential of modern technology (hydraulics, electric lighting) to shape the performance space. From the Duke of Meiningen to Gordon Craig, Adolphe Appia or Terence Gray, this became a major concern of design and direction.

In Meyerhold's 'bio-mechanics' this function of the set was particularly clearly emphasised and exploited: Meyerhold's sets often lacked any representational function and merely provided the geometrical infrastructure for the actors' expressive movement. Here the dynamics of movement became one of the principal signifying systems in the performance.

While the designer's space-creating, dynamic function is more in evidence in the theatre, it is by no means unimportant in cinema: the spectacular movements of crowds in the great epic films, across wide marbled halls, or through narrow city gates, or the movement of hunted victims scrambling up or down narrow spiral staircases in horror pictures, are examples of the same phenomenon, which, however, is often overshadowed by the more spectacular dynamics produced by the mobility of the camera.

On the stage the spatial configuration also has important implications for the *timing* of the performance (another basic element in the perception of its ultimate meaning). For example, the positions of exits and entrances and their accessibility can determine how long it takes the actors to move on and off the stage: the design can thus slow down or speed up the action and decisively influence its basic rhythmic structure. The designer in the theatre thus at least partially performs the editor's function in the cinematic media.

2

The most obvious function of the **set** or **decor** is an informational, iconic one: it 'pictures' the environment against which the action of the drama unfolds, and provides much of the basic expositional information for the spectator's understanding of it by indicating its place and period, the social position of the characters and many other essential aspects of the drama.

On the stage this visual exposition can take the form of painted or three-dimensional sets of varying degrees of verisimilitude from *trompe-l'oeil* to more or less total abstractness.

In the cinematic media it may be provided by a studio set, by back projection or by 'real' backgrounds, 'locations' – these, however real, are also signs in the same sense in which the real human being, the actor, is a sign for a fictional character. Even an actual filmed image of a 'real' street in London or New York becomes a sign for a street in a fictional London or New York. However, a 'real' street in Munich or Helsinki may also play the part of, say, a street in Moscow or Leningrad, or a stretch of sand dunes in Kent may stand for the Western Desert of World

War II. Whether the backgrounds are 'real' or studio constructed, however, does not change their nature as elements of 'design'. The designer, in choosing indoor or outdoor 'locations' is creating them as signifying elements that, in the final analysis, fulfil exactly the same function as those he constructs from his own imagination.

The photographic nature of filmed drama demands a higher degree of realism than the stage. Hence stage sets can rely on a measure of abstraction and may even (as in the example of Meyerhold's 'bio-mechanics') be wholly abstract designs. Such abstract sets clearly lack the iconic element altogether.

Semi-abstract sets, however, are icons, even though they may merely suggest selected features of the reality for which they stand, such as a door-frame for a door, a skeleton outline for a house, etc. For it is of the nature of iconic signs that they do not have to be completely representational. Indeed they can become formalised abstractions (the schematic figures of a man and a woman outside lavatories, the crossed knife and fork in airline timetables) to the point where they gradually merge into hieroglyphics or ideograms and eventually turn into wholly conventional symbols.

In the theatre, paradoxically, real human beings – the actors – can convincingly interact with highly stylised or abstract representations of their environment. They can open schematic or even non-existent doors and freely move between several such schematically suggested environments within a very narrow stage space. Thus *gesture* can become an element of visual design: an actor looking out of an imaginary window, or stooping through an imagined low doorway can actually create those images in the spectator's imagination. Even the modulation of the actor's voice can create space: an actor calling to another character off-stage by 'throwing' his voice as if trying to communicate over a long distance can suggest the immensity of a forest or desert on even the tiniest stage. Here the *principle of the primacy of the actor and action* comes into play. Action can create images, circumscribe space.

In Greek, medieval and Elizabethan drama, to cite but the most familiar examples, the iconic element of the stage set was to a considerable degree suggested by words and gestures, rather than by representational elements.

In the famous prologue to *Henry V* Shakespeare (clearly a highly experienced and conscious practical semiotician of the stage) exhorts his audience to use their imagination, so that the actors, 'ciphers to this great accompt', can 'on your imaginary forces work' and calls upon the spectators to 'piece out our imperfections with your thoughts . . . / think, when we talk of horses that you see them, / printing their proud hoofs i'th' receiving earth: / for 'tis your thoughts that now must deck our kings, / carry them here and there, jumping o'er times, / turning th' accomplishment of many years / into an hour-glass. . . .' In his film of the play Laurence Olivier showed a highly realistic picture of an Elizabethan playhouse in which the Prologue delivered these lines and presented the beginning of the action as seen by the Elizabethan playgoer on that simple stage; then, gradually, to suggest the workings of the audience's imagination, he moved the action in front of flat painted backgrounds and eventually into the full photographic 'reality' of the historical fiction of the play as it might have appeared in the spectators' imagination, only to return, in the end, to the primary, external 'reality' of the Elizabethan playhouse.

In addition to its iconic function the design of the set and costumes also has a powerful symbolic component: the whole mood and meaning of a dramatic performance can be determined by, for example, a **basic colour scheme**, or the decision to adopt a given artistic style – gothic, baroque, futuristic – for both set and costumes.

3

Properties – furniture, tools, instruments and other movable objects present in the dramatic space and used by the characters

– are basically part of the overall design. 'Real' objects, such as tables, chairs, swords used in this context have the same dual aspect as the real people embodying the characters: a chair used in a performance of *Hamlet* is a sign for a fictional chair in the castle of Elsinore in a mythical past and thus has an 'acting role'. At the same time it may be admired for itself, as a splendidly designed object, perhaps even as a real period chair that a spectator might like to acquire. The objects the actors handle, the furniture they use, can also carry important symbolical meaning: a crown may stand for the principle of kingship, as it does most powerfully in Shakespeare's *Richard II*, or a letter may symbolise the hero's downfall or destruction. In melodrama much of the action revolves around such objects charged with symbolic meaning.

Yet, paradoxically, here too complete iconic realism is by no means essential. Objects also obey the principle of the primacy of action in drama. Properties may – on the stage at least, though much less so in photographed drama – be entirely suggested by the actors' action: the characters may be drinking non-existing wine and be handling non-existent tools and yet satisfy the audience's imagination.

4

The use of **light** plays an ever increasing role among the visual signifying systems of drama. It has an obvious iconic function – indicating day and night, sunny and gloomy conditions, etc. and also displays equally obvious symbolic aspects. One of the first great directors to recognise the decisive importance of the potential of electric lighting in the theatre, Max Reinhardt, spoke of the possibility of 'painting' the stage with coloured and modulated light.

But the most important function of light in dramatic performance is deictic. It is the lighting that can direct attention to the focal points of the action, almost literally an 'index' finger pointed at the area of maximum interest. A spotlight may draw attention to the leading character and follow his movements. It may highlight an important object. This is equally true of the stage and of the cinematic media. Indeed, in the cinema the 'lighting cameraman' is one of the dominant creative personalities. On the stage the emergence of sophisticated lighting apparatus, nowadays electronically pre-programmable, has led to more and more intricate nuances of lighting in complex and subtle lighting plots, and to the emergence of the 'lighting designer' as one of the principal creative artists contributing to the performance.

The style and detail of the lighting may – both in the theatre and in the cinematic media – determine the whole 'texture' of the performance, it may keep the action in a chiaroscuro throughout, or, as in the style advocated by Brecht, plunge it into unvarying and glaring clarity (even in scenes taking place at night, when that fact will have to be indicated by properties such as lamps or candles), with all the innumerable variations that lie between these two extremes.

The architectural frame of a performance, the actors and their actions, the sets, costumes and lighting are all visual sign systems that are the fundamentals of all drama. 'Theatron', 'theatre' means a place for looking. In English we speak of going to a 'show', in German a play is a 'Schau-Spiel' ('a play to be looked at'), in French of 'un spectacle'. What do we go to the cinema for? 'Pictures'. And the emphasis in the term television is on the 'vision'. As Goethe puts it in the words of his experienced theatrical entrepreneur in *Faust*:

> Man kommt zu schaun, man will am liebsten sehn.
> Wird vieles vor den Augen abgesponnen,
> So dass die Menge staunend gaffen kann,
> Da habt ihr in der Breite gleich gewonnen,
> Ihr seid ein vielgeliebter Mann.
>
> They come to look, and they love most to see.
> If much is spun about before their eyes,

So that the crowd can in amazement gape
You will have won in breadth immediately,
You'll be a much-beloved man.[1]

That is why I have put a consideration of the visual aspects of drama before what is in most academic discussion usually regarded as its essential constituent, the **words** that are spoken by the characters.

[1] Goethe, *Faust*, 'Vorspiel auf dem Theater'.

VIII

The Signs of Drama: The Words

I

Because the only portion of the dramatic event that leaves a permanent residue for posterity is usually the written record (and because most drama without words, or without a written manuscript, in fact the vast majority of all dramatic performances that ever took place, has left no record at all behind), the text has been regarded by critics and scholars as the essential element of drama. Indeed it has often become synonymous with the whole of drama, something akin to the 'Platonic idea' of the play, with the performance only, at best, an imperfect realisation of that metaphysical entity. That this view is far from universally tenable is made clear by some of the borderline aspects of drama like mime, dumb show or ballet that lack any verbal element, or *commedia dell'arte* where only the basic line of the action is pre-determined and the verbal element, by definition, is therefore fluid; or indeed the silent cinema, where the verbal element was relegated to captions, and where the excellence of the work was in inverse proportion to the number of such captions needed to make it comprehensible.

Insofar as stage drama is concerned, the literary scholar's insistence on the primacy of the text has at least partial validity. To the degree, that is, that the text of a play *can* be read, it *is* literature, and can be analysed and interpreted as if it were poetry, prose or a form of narrative fiction. Yet in texts originally created for performance a proportion of the verbal element will remain obscure without an imaginative reconstruction of the performance that the text was destined to evoke.

Indeed, the permanence of the text (of those performances that have had the good fortune of surviving in manuscript or print) as against the evanescence of the other signifiers gives those stage plays that have survived in print an inestimable advantage over the cinema and television drama. For it allows those texts to be re-incarnated in a very wide variety of different performances in different environments and different epochs, and thus makes them flexible enough to be relatively easily adjusted to successive historical, cultural and technological conditions and to remain viable over several centuries.

The texts of plays as they are available today contain, of course, some indications of the other signifying systems involved, as 'stage directions'. Roman Ingarden differentiates the 'Haupttext' (main text) and the 'Nebentext' (subsidiary text) of a play[1], the latter consisting of the stage-directions, while the former comprises the words that are actually spoken on the stage by the actors. Thus the 'Haupttext' is the only portion of the text that is available to the spectators of a performance as a producer of meaning, while the 'Nebentext' appears in the form of other non-verbal sign systems. But the 'Nebentext' is very often altogether absent (as, for example, in the texts of Greek plays that have come down to us) or extremely scanty and vague (as in the stage directions of Elizabethan drama). In modern performances of these plays, therefore, the director, the designer and the actors create their own, often extremely individual 'Nebentexts'. In the mechanically reproducible forms of drama (cinema and television) the 'Haupttext' and 'Nebentext' are indissolubly welded together. In published versions of screenplays the 'Nebentext' occupies a far larger proportion of the script than in stage-plays, which is one of the reasons it is so much more difficult to enjoy reading the printed versions of

[1] Roman Ingarden, 'Von den Funktionen der Sprache im Theaterschauspiel', Appendix to *Das Literarische Kunstwerk*, 2nd ed., Tübingen: Max Niemayer, 1960, p. 403.

screen- or television plays. The visual elements predominate in those forms of drama with the result that verbal accounts of the visuals lack the evocative power descriptive passages hold in narrative literature. The melding of text and performance is the reason why 're-makes' of the same scenario in the cinema result in totally different works with often vastly different meanings, evidence that the words that are actually spoken – and appear on the printed page of plays handed down from past epochs – are far from being the whole of the drama, that the texts even of far more verbal stage-plays by no means represent the 'Platonic idea' of the spectacle, but are merely an important ingredient that may or may not be the ultimate determinant of its meaning for the spectators of a given performance.

2

In spite of these caveats, the text of a dramatic work does of course contain a plethora of immensely important meaning-producing elements. There is the **basic lexical meaning** of the words themselves, their syntactic meaning, their referential meaning to circumstances in the 'real' world (for example in a political drama that aims at commenting on a social situation), the whole gamut, in short, of the ways in which speech conveys meaning in daily life. The words of dramatic dialogue conform to all we know about the use of language as a medium of human intercourse. They are 'speech acts' as they have been described and analysed by J. L. Austin[2] and J. R. Searle[3], as well as vehicles for the transmission of factual and emotional information. In addition, in drama, there are the meaning-producing elements of the **style** of the text: whether it is in prose or verse, or in a mixture of the two, whether the style of the text aims at a high or low type of linguistic utterance. The words also serve to

[2] J. L. Austin, *How to do Things with Words*, London: Oxford University Press, 1962.
[3] J. R. Searle, *Speech Acts: An Essay in the Philosophy of Language*, Cambridge: Cambridge University Press, 1969.

individualise characters by giving each of them his personal speech-pattern and vocabulary, his regional dialect or professional jargon, etc. The verbal text also produces meaning through the overall **structure of the dialogue**. It embodies the 'narrative' technique by which the action is structured through the sequence of scenes; the dynamic of contrasts between long and short, violent and quiet segments, repetition and assonance; the rhythms inherent in the dialogue, the pauses and silences which, even if they are not indicated by stage directions ('Nebentext') are, in skilfully written texts overwhelmingly strongly imposed by the structure of words and sentence rhythms; and by the subtle 'timing' of the dialogue itself.

All speech in drama, moreover, produces meaning on several levels. While communicating a given meaning from one character to another, the same sentence will, in addition, convey another, and perhaps, dramatically more important meaning to the audience. Character A (say: Iago) may tell character B (say: Othello) that he respects him, but the audience, having heard his previous utterances, will know that he is lying and that a sinister train of events has been initiated. The words spoken between the characters always contain another charge of meaning for the audience. When, at the opening of Ibsen's *A Doll's House*, Nora Hellmer gives the porter a crown after he has carried the Christmas tree upstairs for her and asked only fifty øre for his services, and then tells him to 'keep the change',[4] her words also tell the audience that she is a generous, a recklessly generous person, as well as a number of other things: her social position, need to assert herself etc. which will later be clarified by the action. Every word of dramatic dialogue thus carries (at least) a double charge: the factual meaning of the words, on the one hand; the information they yield about the character of the speaker on the other. The decoding of this secondary string of meaning, moreover, is a continuous process – with each new line of dialogue putting an additional touch to the character

[4] Ibsen, *A Doll's House*, Act I.

portrait that is being built up, with all its dialectic of inner contradictions and inconsistencies.

In Ibsen's text Nora actually says 'keep the change'. But in performance this sentence is not essential. She could just as well indicate her intention by a slight gesture, by handing the change back to the porter, or by a mere smile. This emphasises one of the basic distinctions between a literary and a dramatic text. The dramatic text is always incomplete. As Ingarden points out[5] drama represents its world by 1) events that are wholly indicated by visual and other means, 2) by elements which are indicated both verbally and visually and 3) by events that are indicated only in words, as, for example, narrations of events that have happened outside the spatial or temporal ambit of the action.

What must be emphasised here is the primacy of the first category of indicators (the non-verbal ones) over the text. Drama is essentially mimetic *action*. If there is a contradiction between the words and the action, the action prevails. A good example of this is the ending of *Waiting For Godot*, when the verbal exhortation 'let's go' is contradicted by the action indicated in the 'Nebentext': 'they don't move'. (Here, incidentally, the literary bias of the critical vocabulary shows itself: the 'Nebentext' is in fact always more important than the 'Haupttext'.) Whether it is the assassin who speaks loving words while sinking his dagger in his victim's body, or the dying man who assures his friends that he feels well, the action always overrules the words and, indeed, puts the words into an ironical context, revealing their impotence in the face of events that are beyond words.

Drama being action, the verbal element in drama must also function primarily as **action**. The words that are uttered receive their meaning less by what their lexical or syntactic content expresses than by what they *do* to the characters to whom they are addressed or, in monologic passages, to the characters who

[5] Ingarden, op. cit. p. 405

speak them (think of Hamlet's 'Oh what a rogue and peasant slave am I' soliloquy by which he clarifies his own mind and conceives a new plan of action). Soliloquies and monologic speech can be of two kinds: either the character debates with himself, with the audience merely overhearing his innermost thoughts; or he actually addresses the audience directly. In the first case the character is acting upon himself ('changing his mind'), in the second he is acting upon the audience.

When the words spoken are in contradiction to the action of the characters, they, of course, are also part of the action, revealing its complexity and mixed motivation. Where simple wordless action is sufficient to indicate what is happening, words are redundant. In fact economy of words is something like a dramatic Occam's Razor.

One of the greatest teachers of acting in our time, Jacques Lecoq, starts his students off with 'situations' in which they have to improvise responses to each other in various social roles (for example, guests at a party who have not yet been introduced to each other). For as long as possible they have to interact in silence, only when words become absolutely essential are they allowed to speak. This embodies one of the basic principles of the 'economy' of drama: anything that is expressible without words should do without them. This, indeed, is the reason why there is less need for dialogue in the cinema. The camera can convey far more information by its 'deictic' action than is possible on the stage.

3

The meaning of verbal utterances by the characters in drama can never be merely analysed in isolation from the dramatic context in which it occurs and the *action* it represents. As action, however, always springs from character, the meaning of a dramatic utterance must also always be understood in the light of the character from whom it emanates. A dramatist can never make a statement in his own name, utter his own opinion within the dialogue (or the monologues, or 'asides' spoken by the characters). When playwrights from Shakespeare to Brecht want to put over their own comment on the action they have to resort to prologues, epilogues or songs presented by actors who have visibly stepped outside their characters. Even those 'narrative' passages spoken by characters like the Storyteller in *The Caucasian Chalk Circle* can not be perceived as 'wholly' the author's opinion. There must always be the subjectivity of the character (in this case a Caucasian folk poet) taken into account. In the cinema a genuine authorial comment must also be confined to 'voice-overs' external to the action, or captions as used by the silent cinema and by directors with a 'Brechtian' bias like Godard.

Nor can any words spoken by a character in drama thus be taken at their face-value. They are always the product of the character, the character's motivations and the situation in which he finds himself. The audience is constantly compelled to question these motivations and to subject them to continuous analysis in the light of the developing situations. An assertion that is made can be proved or discredited by subsequent events. Much here also depends on the often-discussed dialectic between what the characters know or do not know and what the audience knows that the characters may not know. If, in Dürrenmatt's often quoted example[6], two characters are having coffee, the matter becomes dramatic according to whether the audience knows that one of the cups is poisoned, or even both, and either one or both characters do not know it. The words spoken by these two characters in such a situation may be of the utmost triviality. It is the situation that charges them with a maximum of meaning. This type of 'dramatic irony' has been one of the most ancient devices of drama, from Oedipus' insistence on learning the full truth; to the tensions arising out of the audience's knowledge that Laertes' foil is poisoned; or Wallen-

[6] F. Dürrenmatt, 'Theaterprobleme' in *Theater-Schriften und Reden*, Zürich, Arche, 1966, p. 111–12.

stein's seemingly trivial remark that he intends to sleep long this night, when the audience already knows that he is about to be assassinated.

4

The notion of the 'subtext' that has become so familiar since Chekhov merely emphasises the complex palimpsest of meanings constituted by a dramatic text. It is not only the playwright who can never express his opinion or message in drama, because it will always merely be the opinion of one character. The characters themselves, particularly in post-Chekhovian drama, may well rarely say what they really mean simply because people in real life frequently avoid being too direct, and interpersonal problems are only rarely solved by talking about them. As the poet Hofmannsthal put it when discussing one of his libretti with the composer Richard Strauss; 'Has it never struck you that in real life nothing is ever decided by talking it out? One is never so alone, so convinced of the impossibility of resolving a situation as after one has tried to resolve it by talking'[7].

It is from the dialectical interplay between the situation as it has developed from the chain of previous situations, on the one hand, and the words that *are* spoken, on the other, that the underlying unspoken thoughts and emotions of the characters – the subtext – ultimately emerge for the attentive and perceptive spectator who has often instinctively mastered the art of decoding such a subtle interplay of signs.

Thus the 'meaning' of the words spoken in drama, in the last analysis, derives (beyond its purely lexical, syntactical, referential, metric and other meanings open to a purely literary interpretation) from a consideration of *who* does *what* with those words *to whom* under *which circumstances*. Or, more concisely, in drama the meaning of the words derives ultimately from the

[7] H. v. Hofmannsthal, 'Die aegyptische Helena' in *Prosa IV*, Frankfurt: S. Fischer, 1955, p. 441.

situation from which they spring.

This also is the source of that 'poetry of the stage' – and the screen – which endows the most trivial everyday utterance with such overwhelming emotional force (Lear's 'Pray you undo this button'; Michèle Morgan's 'Qu'il est difficile, vivre!' in Marcel Carné's *Quai Des Brumes*). And it is precisely the verbal economy of the utterance, in a context defined by non-verbal sign systems as well as by the 'situation' of the utterance in the sequence of events, which gives such words their immense impact.

Drama can thus be seen as a sequence, a continuum of *situations*. This points up another essential distinction between a dramatic and a literary text: in performance a dramatic text exists and unfolds in time as well as space, whereas the read text remains outside a rigid time frame. While it is possible to interrupt or put down a literary text that one is reading, one of the chief distinctions of a dramatic text in performance is its relentless and irreversible progression from situation to situation within each of its basic structural elements (scenes, acts, sequences). A dramatic performance thus becomes a very definite 'structure-in-time' with its own important characteristics: pace, rhythm, variation in pitch and loudness and the formal patterns such variations create.

It is this time-dimension that drama shares with its sister performance-art: music.

IX

The Signs of Drama: Music and Sound

Nietzsche spoke of the 'birth of tragedy from the spirit of music'. Whether one is prepared to follow him the whole way in his poetic vision, it is an undoubted fact that the origins of drama lie in a shadowy past when ritual, dance and the singing of hymns or the recitation of epic poems had not yet been wholly differentiated.

Hence it is not surprising that music has always played an important part as a signifying system in dramatic performance. In Greek tragedy and in the ancient comedy there can be little doubt that the choral odes were both sung and danced.

Those types of drama that dispense with music altogether form a relatively small proportion of the total mass of performed drama throughout its history; many more have used and still use inserted songs, dances and background mood music. One only has to think of the omnipresent background music in cinema and television drama.

Opera, undoubtedly a form of drama, owes its origin to the assumption by Renaissance scholars that the dialogue of Greek tragedy was sung rather than spoken. While today the text in opera tends merely to form a 'pre-text' for the music (and is often well-nigh unintelligible), its musical notation can be seen as having sprung from an attempt at fixing that all-important sign-system of acting, the vocal enunciation and delivery of the text. The music that accompanies the singing also provides a powerful 'subtext' by indicating the mood, the hidden thoughts and emotions of thc characters.

Wagner's idea of drama as a 'Gesamtkunstwerk', in which all the arts – that is, the signifying systems of drama, verbal, musical and visual – would be wholly fused, is the ultimate expression of this extreme view of the dramatic function of music. Yet by its very extremism Wagner's concept has proved too narrow: many of the important social and artistic functions of drama lie outside the scope of what such music-drama could provide. Wagner himself acknowledged this by considering his type of music-drama as an exceptional festive ritual event rather than as an ingredient of the daily and continuing cultural needs of a society.

On a more lowly plane music performs a variety of vital roles in the signifying system of dramatic performance: it can provide an important structural element with inserted songs breaking the flow of the action and punctuating moments of deep feeling, as in the plays of Shakespeare; it can provide the rhythmic skeleton for pure movement in scenes involving dance (with ballet as an extreme case and the dance numbers of operetta, musical comedy or musical cinema near the same end of the spectrum); and, particularly in cinema and television, it can form an almost constant background, often barely perceived by the conscious mind of the audience, but precisely because of this, even more powerful in establishing the mood and meaning of the action. This latter use of music directly derives from the melodrama of nineteenth-century popular theatre, but also goes back to the sung choruses of Ancient Greece and the music accompanying liturgical drama.

In the foregoing examples music acts in concert with the basic line of the action and the text. Brecht, on the other hand, conceived the use of music – as of other signifying systems of drama – as antithetic, in a dialectical relationship to each other. He wanted the songs, for example, to break the action and to force the actor to step outside his role while performing them; and he also wanted the tune to provide an ironic commentary on the words rather than 'expressing' their meaning – so that the contrast between the cynicism of the words and the sentimentality of the music, say, in the song of the men waiting in line to be admitted to the brothel in *Mahagonny*, would provide a dialectical image of the hypocrisy and false consciousness of a society based on greed.

Brecht also wanted to use music as a mnemonic device, by which the moral and political lessons of the action could – very much in the manner in which the Greek chorus drew the lessons of the events of the play – be made more easily remembered. In this, as in so many other aspects of his thinking, he was merely following the tradition of Austrian and Bavarian folk theatre, which had always relied on tunes that would imprint themselves on the mind and ultimately led to popular forms like Viennese operetta (and on to the modern musical) that relied on just such compulsively memorable melodies.

Non-musical sound also has played its part in dramatic performance from the earliest times: claps of thunder and the howling of wind could be powerfully imitated by simple mechanical means. Since the coming of recorded sound the scope of sound effects has been immensely widened. In the theatre stereophonic sound can simulate the whole gamut of natural sounds from bird songs to earthquakes, while in the cinema elaborate quadraphonic apparatus can flood the audience with sounds from all directions and produce veritable orgies of dramatic power in, for instance, 'disaster movies'. Sound effects of this type are 'iconic' because directly representational. But they can also occasionally be used symbolically, witness the heartbeats of dying characters and the ticking of clocks in cinema – or the famous sound of a breaking string at the end of Chekhov's *Cherry Orchard*.

X

The Signs of Stage and Screen

I

All the sign systems already discussed are present in various combinations in forms of drama that are staged 'live' as well as those that are mechanically and photographically recorded. Ballet or mime (on stage or screen) may lack the verbal element, some abstract or minimalist works (on stage or screen) may do without props or elaborately designed sets or lighting, or without an element of music: different combinations of all these sign systems are nevertheless imaginable in both live and mechanically recorded performances.

Yet there is a fundamental dichotomy between the live and recorded forms of dramatic performance, a division which has led, in the case of film criticism, to the view that the cinema and the theatre are fundamentally different art forms.

The argument advanced here, on the other hand, is that while the differences are very real and must be fully understood, the cinematic types of drama share so large a gamut of signifying systems with the live theatre that the differences between them can be usefully and fruitfully accommodated within the single concept of 'drama' or 'dramatic performance'; and that, indeed, criticism of both basic types of drama can benefit by being seen in that context; that, in fact some useful insights might be derived from considering their contrasting characteristics.

2

As regards the 'live' theatre its only truly distinctive feature, and one that constitutes an immense advantage vis-à-vis the mechanically reproduced forms of drama is its ability to establish an immediate inter-action between performers and audience, a continuous feed-back of reactions.

That the performance unrolls itself in the presence of the audience, that it allows spontaneous modifications of its pre-set and rehearsed elements in the light of the actual circumstances prevailing during the performance, that unforeseen inspirations as well as mistakes can occur, all these factors enhance the excitement of the event for performers as well as spectators. Even more important is the fact that the reaction of the spectators can be made instantly manifest to the performers, by their laughter, their silence with bated breath, their spontaneous applause, or in certain forms of oriental drama by loud exhortation or verbal encouragement. In the light of such reactions the actors can immediately modify and adapt their performance.

Audiences vary from performance to performance, owing to a multitude of factors: a full house produces a more receptive mood than an empty one; bad weather outside, the political situation, or simply the presence of large cohesive groups of spectators (coach parties from the suburbs, foreign tourists) modify the collective individuality of the audience, its reactions as a crowd subject to the specific characteristics of a mass-psychological entity. Actors touring with a play from city to city are, moreover, convinced that the quickness of reaction, the readiness to respond of audiences varies from place to place. The actors sense these specific characteristics of audiences very quickly and will adjust their performance to them. Thus certain audiences may be slower to provoke into laughter than others. The actors will immediately underline and intensify the elements that they regard as the basis of a stronger reaction: they will 'push the jokes harder'. Experienced performers have learned to gauge the crowd response to the point where, as the saying goes, 'they can hold the audience in the palm of their hands'. Experienced and skilled actors can subdue the audience as the matador subdues the bull.

This phenomenon amounts to a continuous process of feed-back between the performers and the audience: by reacting to the audience, the actors modify the audience's reaction and that modified reaction, in turn, is felt by the actors – and so on.

Equally important is the fact that this is not merely a two-way traffic. Each member of the audience also reacts to the reaction of the other members of the audience: if the person next to me laughs loudly, I shall probably, because laughter is contagious, laugh more loudly or intensely myself. (This feed-back effect between audience members is, of course, also present in the cinema, where the performance is already fixed once and for all, but audience reactions vary spontaneously from one showing to the next. In television, which is usually watched by isolated individuals or very small groups, the feed-back between audience members is further reduced – one of the reasons why television is forced to resort to studio audiences or 'canned laughter'.)

That the multiple feed-back effect of live performance is of inestimable value in enhancing the experience of the event, both for the actors and the spectators, is beyond doubt. Yet although, of course, the heightened intensity of the experience, the greater degree of concentration it produces in the individual spectator, may contribute to the spectator's ability to derive meaning from the performance, it hardly constitutes a distinct system of signs in the sense in which semiotics uses the term. This leaves us with the additional meaning-generating abilities of the two cinematic dramatic media – the cinema and television.

3

The mechanically reproduced and photographic forms of drama – the feature film and the television play – differ from live dramatic performance in that the spectator in the mechanically transmitted media has no direct contact with the performers, that their work has to be brought to him through the mediation of the camera.

Insofar as drama of this type tends to be recorded on film or videotape – live television drama has become exceedingly rare – the dramatic action, moreover, has already happened outside the spectator's own time-frame. It thus lacks a certain element of the unexpected, the spontaneous event – or, indeed, potential mishap – which enhances the excitement of live performance.

In the theatre the spectator is presented with a predetermined, given space, the stage. This space may be fixed, rigidly circumscribed and static, surrounded by a proscenium arch and thus resembling a picture within a frame; or it may be an open arena; or, indeed, in 'environmental' productions, it may surround both spectators and actors; it may be used to represent and accommodate different locations, environments, 'sets', made palpably visible or merely imagined (as in the Elizabethan theatre). But that space itself, whatever shape it takes, will always be a 'given'. It is static, it remains, constantly and unmoving in front of, or around, the spectator.

Within this space, which constantly remains within the range of his focused and peripheral vision, he can look wherever he feels the focus of the action resides at any given moment. As the spectator in the theatre focuses his attention, he has to make choices as to where he will look at any stage of the performance: at the hero's action, or the villain's re-action, up at Juliet, or down at Romeo in the balcony scene, and so on. In that respect the spectator in a live performance does what the camera does for him in the cinematic forms of drama: he creates a sequence of close-ups and long-shots, a freely chosen 'montage' of focused images. At times when it was the fashion for members of the audience to use 'opera glasses', they quite consciously created 'close-ups' of the leading players or singers for themselves.

The same process goes on, even with the naked eye.

Thus, in the theatre the spectator's eye roaming at will from character to character, from one part of the stage to another, assembles a sequence of different angles of vision, of different picture-segments, which creates its own dynamic (as indeed the viewer of a painting creates a kind of dramatic unfolding of the picture by moving his glance along its various axes which the painter in deciding on its composition has cunningly provided).

In this respect the difference between the cinematic and the live dramatic media merely derives from the fact that the spectator is freer to compose his own 'editing' of the action.

The director of a film (abetted by the editor) tries to replicate the choices – where to look at any moment in the dramatic action – that an ideal spectator would make; but, in addition, he has the power to compel the spectator to look at certain things and to restrict his ability to look at others, which he, as director, wants to conceal or withold. As André Bazin says:

> . . . normal editing is a compromise between three ways of possibly analyzing reality:
>
> 1) *A purely logical and descriptive analysis* (the weapon used in the crime lying beside the corpse). 2) *A psychological analysis* from within the film, namely one that fits the point of view of one of the protagonists in a given situation. An example of this would be the glass of milk that may possibly be poisoned that Ingrid Bergman has to drink in *Notorious*. . . . 3) *Finally a psychological analysis from the point of view of spectator interest*, either a spontaneous interest or one provoked by the director thanks precisely to this analysis. An example of this would be the handle of a door turning unseen by the criminal who thinks he is alone ('Look out', the children used to shout to the Guignol whom the policeman is about to surprise).[1]

Point 3) of this analysis highlights the close analogy between

[1] A. Bazin, *What is Cinema?*, vol. 1. Berkeley: University of California Press, 1967, pp. 91/2.

the theatre spectator's choice – guided by the director's use of light, grouping of characters, movement etc. – as to where to direct his attention, and the film director's deictic use of the camera. Bazin's final, quite natural use of the analogy with the Punch and Judy show, the most basic case of 'live' drama, clearly shows that in this respect he does not find any fundamental difference between staged and filmed drama.

A much more decisive difference between live and cinematic drama lies in the fundamental distinction between the theatrical and the cinematic space. Whereas the stage (whether of the 'peep-show' type, an open arena or 'in the round') confronts the spectator throughout the performance and is its basic 'given', the cinema or television screens are doors through which the spectator freely enters a space which is infinitely variable and constantly changing. The spectator in the theatre 'confronts' a space, the spectator in the cinema and television 'is sucked into' and propelled through a sequence of different spaces. Because the camera acts as the spectator's eye, the spectator enters any space into which the camera takes him: he speeds along in a car, runs in and out of houses, approaches and recedes from objects. This increases the spectator's 'mobility in space'. He can be propelled to any point the director wants him to be.

On the other hand his total control over the spectator's eye through his control of the camera also allows the director to *restrict* the spectator's vision at will: he can show him the hand of the murderer, without revealing the face which would give away the murderer's identity, he can concentrate on the feet of a milling crowd without showing us on what street, or in what room those people are moving.

The director uses the camera thus in a compellingly *deictic* role – it takes the spectator by the scruff of his neck, drags him into the action and points him and his eyes at the spaces, people and objects the director has decided he must look at.

Not only does the camera guide the spectator's eye from point to point, making him look more closely at a detail or step back and take a wider view – providing, in other words, a number of different 'shots' – but the creator of the cinematic drama also determines the dynamic of the way in which each partial image is fused into a continuous, meaningfully linked sequence, with its own rhythm and narrative line.

So, what in the theatre remained the spectator's freely (albeit semi-subconsciously) selected assemblage of a sequence of visual impressions through his shifting focus of attention, becomes, in the cinematic forms of drama, a carefully judged and pre-determined artistic process, a principle of narration. In this process the selection of viewpoints ('shots') and their rhythmic fusion (through the 'panning' or 'travelling' of the camera), followed by their assemblage on film or videotape into a continuous, carefully regulated and judged sequence – in other words, 'editing', or 'montage' of pre-recorded images – becomes an additional, immensely powerful generator of meaning. Hence most of the thinking about the aesthetics of the cinematic media revolves around the techniques arising out of this *deictic* function of the camera and the rhythmics and dynamics of fusing its images into a carefully controlled stream of visual statements.

Film theoreticians tend to distinguish between, on the one hand, the 'mise-en-scène' – which comprises all the sign systems that create meaning on the stage and is the *given* that is being photographed – and, on the other, the 'art of the director', which involves the selection and composition of 'shots'. As a result the 'mise-en-scène' (being essentially identical with the methods of staging in the theatre) tends to get short shrift in contemporary film-criticism, with the acting, design, and above all the script being treated as secondary elements.

It is true that the director's and editor's influence on the acting, for example, is considerable. Weak moments can be eliminated, and 'montage' can achieve powerful effects merely through suggestive juxtaposition of shots. Kuleshov's famous experiment, in which the same, neutral close-up of a face seems to change its expression when juxtaposed with other – pleasant or unpleasant – shots, is often cited in this connection.

Nevertheless the concentration of the various schools of film aesthetics on the specifically 'filmic' aspects of cinematic drama has had the consequence of devaluing the contribution of the other sign systems. The 'auteur' theory of cinema, for example, which postulates the director as the sole creator of the film and tends to regard the contribution of writer, designer, cameraman and editor and all the other creative artists involved as secondary, not only patently falsifies an existing state of affairs, as most films are the product of a multitude of more or less fortuitously assembled contributors, but has led to the comparative neglect of the contribution of all other artists – writers, designers and above all actors – in the more intellectually ambitious forms of film criticism. In the real world of film-making, it could well be argued, the central factor in the creation of a given film is much more frequently the 'star', whose 'bankable' presence in the scheme generates the money that makes its production possible, and whose influence is bound to pervade the entire production process and many of the director's choices.

Moreover, it may well be the influence of the overvaluation of the director's function that has led to the notorious under-valuing of the writer's contribution in the cinema.

It is significant that in the television medium, where, for economic reasons, much less time and effort can be expended on re-taking the same scene over and over again, and where there is even less time to edit the material, considerable writers like Harold Pinter, Tom Stoppard, David Mercer, Samuel Beckett, have been able to create drama of a high order of literary and artistic integrity, presented in a cinematic form. Indeed, in the case of Beckett, the 'auteur' concept works more convincingly than in the cinema: here the 'auteur' is the writer, who is enabled to give concrete form to his imagination by being allowed to direct his own text. Even in the cinema itself some major masterpieces have resulted from the work of directors who wrote their own scripts or of writers who have had the good fortune of being able to direct – or otherwise control – the realisation of their dramatic ideas – Keaton, Chaplin, Orson Welles, Jean Cocteau and Woody Allen are cases in point here.

4

The signifying systems that derive from the deictic role of the camera and the techniques of **montage** and **editing** have been explored in detail by the semioticians of the cinema, who have formulated the 'grammar' and 'syntax' of the use of longshots and close-ups and their combination, the different implications of a sharp cut and a slow crossfade, single static shots held for a long time as against a dynamic montage of short images, or a rhythmically controlled mixture of both, as in the famous murder scene in the shower in Hitchcock's *Psycho*.

While certain techniques of this kind – like the slow dissolve that precedes a flashback – have become conventionalised into instantly recognisable 'symbolic' devices immediately understood by the public, it is, even here, somewhat problematic to talk about a 'language' with a fixed 'grammar': new and unconventional ways of handling these techniques by innovative directors may well use them in entirely new ways and produce different meanings. Indeed, that is the very essence of creativeness in this as in any other medium, so that too rigid a codification of the 'meanings' of specific techniques might become as stultifying as the strict application of the three unities in French classical drama.

Moreover, fashions change: the 'montage' of seemingly unrelated shots, once regarded as one of the essential expressive powers of the medium under the influence of the great Russian pioneers like Eisenstein and Pudovkin, and still used by Chaplin in the juxtaposition of a herd of sheep and a crowd of workers in the opening of *Modern Times*, has now become decidedly old-fashioned.

The ease with which cinematic drama can switch locale and scenery, its facility in moving forward and backward in time has in turn had its influence on live drama – another clear sign of the deep underlying unity of the dramatic media.

Techniques like the flashback, the dynamic montage of long and short scenes, frequent change of the place of the action, the use of recorded voice-overs, or narrators who are present on stage and weave in and out of the action, have become commonplace in contemporary stage drama. While these developments may appear revolutionary after a long period dominated by classical and naturalistic conventions which insisted on a strict three- or five-act structure or the convention of the missing fourth wall, the cinema here merely renewed links with the much freer medieval and Elizabethan conventions of drama, which also used a montage of short scenes, as well as narration (as Shakespeare did in *Pericles* or in *Henry V* and *The Winter's Tale* to cite but the most obvious examples).

Yet it is undoubtedly under the influence of the cinema – and radio which uses narrators with even greater frequency – that the techniques of stage drama have been opened up and freed from the constraints of the 'well-made-play'. Audiences used to the cinema will now readily accept epic drama relying on complex levels of narration like Brecht's *The Caucasian Chalk Circle*, or reversals of the chronological time sequence as in Pinter's *Betrayal* or Caryl Churchill's *Top Girls*.

What the theatre retains as its own peculiar strength is its ability to suggest real objects through symbolic action: an actor can mime drinking from a non-existent glass or using a non-existent gun on the stage, while the cinema owing to its photographic nature and hence its need for greater realism is compelled to use real objects. On the other hand the deictic nature of the camera, its ability to point to a small object by moving it into close-up has greatly increased the cinema's ability to use real objects in the role of symbols. The cinema can create the visual equivalent of the Wagnerian 'Leitmotiv' by associating objects, or even whole landscapes, with particular ideas or emotions.

5

Some of the most important distinctions between the three visual dramatic media – the stage, cinema and television – derive from the differing conditions under which they are viewed by their audiences.

Here the cinema and the live theatre share – as against television – the important characteristic that their products are watched by crowds assembled in darkened rooms: thus the reactions of their audiences are governed by the phenomena of collective 'mass' rather than individual psychology. Moreover, in both cases, the performance is perceived as an event in itself, an occasion for the sake of which one has made an effort (leaving home, buying a ticket etc.), whereas television is casually entered into, and equally casually opted out of.

In the theatre the audience is in the presence of the purveyors of the communication – the actors. This sets off the complex process of feed-back between the audience and the actors and among members of the audience mentioned earlier.

In the cinema the feedback between audience and performers is eliminated, but the perception by the audience of its own reaction remains extremely powerful. Here the ability of the medium to direct the attention of all audience members to the same details by the manipulation of their viewpoint actually strengthens the uniformity of the audience's response. Hence, for example, the hysterical bursts of laughter that can be aroused by the best of filmed farce.

In television drama this mass-psychological response is totally absent. Not only does the television audience lack the surrounding crowd, they are also free from the constraints upon people sitting in a darkened, crowded room and therefore more or less compelled to sit through the whole performance. The television audience can leave the performance at the flick of a switch. Hence the much lower intensity of response to television drama, hence also the frantic concentration of television drama upon suspense-enhancing effects, the insistence on packing suspense-provoking incidents into the first minutes of a play – and, in comedy, the use of studio audience or canned laughter, in order to exploit the contagious nature of laughter in the hope that it will make even solitary viewers join in.

In the theatre and cinema where the spectator is part of a crowd and thus is affected by mass psychology he nevertheless also remains his individual self with his or her own individual cultural baggage and personal tastes and preoccupations. There is a tension between these two polarities. The contagion of the hilarity around him (or her) may make an individual laugh about a joke he (or she) has not wholly grasped, the wave of sentimentality engulfing the mass may make him (or her) weep about something which, if exposed to it alone, he might regard as sentimental twaddle.

Television, being constantly available on tap in the home, is perceived by the audience as a continuous stream of entertainment. Thus each individual item or programme will inevitably receive some additional and unintended meaning by being juxtaposed with other items that precede or follow it. The perception of a news report about a space flight will affect and be affected by a science fiction film before or after it, a political play by the news that follows or precedes it.

The paradox here is that, in the case of commercial television, moreover, this continuum is itself constantly fragmented and interrupted by extraneous material in the form of advertisements. Hence the production of 'meaning', the purveying of subtler types of dramatic information, is more difficult on television, and frequently leads to more insistent pointing, more heavy underlining of semiotic information in television film and drama. Hence also, as everything has to be done to hold the attention of a very volatile audience, the tendency towards more and more violence, more and more sensational content in television drama made to be directed at the audiences of commercial television.

Technical developments which will increase the sharpness of the picture and make ever larger television screens available will also tend to bring television drama ever closer to the cinema. On small screens with a relatively small number of lines in the signal, longshots did not convey sufficient detail so that television drama tended to concentrate on full and medium close-ups.

The advent of the distribution of videotaped films constitutes a new aspect of the gradual merging of cinematic and televisual drama. Taped cinema films are seen as small screens by small numbers of people in non-theatrical conditions. Hence an important aspect of the creation of meaning in the cinema is being lost. On the other hand the film will unfold without commercial interruption on the home screen, and the viewing of the film will – if it has been bought or rented – have more of a sense of occasion than a casually turned on television play.

6

If we now try to systematise the different elements that create the first – denotational – level of the 'meaning' of a dramatic performance, we might arrive at the following tabulation:

Sign systems common to all dramatic media

1. Framing systems outside the drama proper
    a. Architectural framework and ambiance surrounding the performance
    b. Title, generic description, pre-publicity
    c. Prologue, title sequence, epilogue etc.

2. Sign systems at the actor's disposal
    a. Personality, balance of 'casting'
    b. Delivery of the text
    c. Facial expression

d. Gesture, body language
e. Movement in space
f. Make-up, hairstyle
g. Costume

3. Visual sign systems
   a. Basic spatial configuration
   b. Visual representation of locale
   c. Colour scheme
   d. Properties
   e. Lighting

4. The text
   a. Basic lexical, syntactic, referential meaning of the words
   b. Style – high/low, prose/verse etc.
   c. Individualisation of characters
   d. Overall structure – rhythm – timing
   e. Text as action – subtext

5. Aural sign systems
   a. Music
   b. Non-musical sounds

Sign Systems confined to Cinema and Television

1. Sign systems derived from camera work
   a. Static shots: long-shot, medium and full-close-up
   b. Panning shots
   c. Travelling shots
   d. Slow motion, and accelerated motion shots

2. Sign systems derived from the linking of shots
   1. Dissolve
   2. Crossfade
   3. Split screen
   4. Sharp cut

3. The sign system of editing
   1. Montage
   2. Use of the rhythmic flow of images

Compared to Kowzan's 13 sign systems (applicable to live drama) in five groups, this amounts to a total of 22 different sign systems common to all dramatic media grouped in five, but slightly different clusters, plus three clusters comprising 10 additional semiotic systems confined to the cinematic media.

All such tables, as all attempts at a systematisation of such complex phenomena, must be highly tentative, especially in this field, where the overlap between, and the mutual merging of, the distinct systems constantly complicates matters.

Costume and make-up belong to design as much as to the actor, the designer influences the movement and thus the acting of the actor, the lighting designer's work overlaps and supports that of the set designer, the text dictates gesture and movement, and in the cinematic media the camera and the editing process greatly influence the significance of the elements of mise-en-scène.

These, then, are the means, the tools by which the originators of a dramatic performance can establish their characters, paint their background and environment, tell their story.

Yet there is always more to a story than merely its basic outline. Once the actual, factual, *denotational* level has been established, other levels of meaning intervene. The originators of the performance (writer, director, designer, composer) may ultimately aim at those higher levels – the moral, political, philosophical message they want to convey – but those levels must firmly be based on the denotational meaning of the signs they have presented to their audience.

Yet the individual signs are only the raw material of the creation of significance and meaning. The individual sign systems we have analysed combine to create signifying structures of a higher order.

XI

Structure as Signifier

I

The different sign systems deployed to create meaning in dramatic performance, enumerated and described in the previous chapters, are, of course, never perceived each by itself, separately and distinctly, or indeed, consciously.

The separate analysis of each of these 'languages' (and the analogies with verbal language should always be treated with caution) can yield some important practical and theoretical insights. But it must always be recognised that all these individual 'signs' are always part of an organic whole, in which the different signs and sign systems constantly inter-act, re-inforce each other or create new meanings out of the ironic contrast, or inner tension, between two or several of them deployed simultaneously; and that the full meaning of a dramatic performance must of necessity always emerge from the total impact of these complex, multilayered structures of interwoven and interdependent signifiers.

In his *Poetics* Aristotle speaks of six elements of tragedy – clearly also applicable to all drama. The first three he describes as constituting *the means and manner of the mimesis*: Diction (lexis), which roughly corresponds to our clusters of sign systems used by the actor and the verbal text; then Spectacle, i.e. the visual element (opsis); and thirdly the Musical element (melos – most important in Greek drama as the choral passages were almost certainly sung). [The only sign system we have focused on which is not covered by Aristotle is that of the external framing and introductory devices, which did not play any great part in Greek drama.]

Aristotle's second triad of the elements of drama concerns the *objects represented* by these means: they are: Plot (mythos); Character (ethe) and Thought, or the intellectual, or religious, content of the drama (dianoia).

It will be readily recognised that the second triad – the subject or content of the drama – is created through the combination and accumulation of the individual signs and sign systems supplied by the first triad comprising the 'means' by which the dramatic illusion is created. Thus the appearance, make-up, voice, verbal delivery, costume, gestures and movement of the actor will coalesce into the totality of the 'character' he is representing; and the interaction of characters thus constituted, in turn, will, over the duration of the performance, merge into the plot or 'fable' that is being shown, through their dialogues, confrontations, hostile or loving contacts, their movement towards or away from each other within the changing locations indicated by the settings of the drama. And then, on an even higher plane of synthesis, out of the interaction of character and plot, there will, for the spectator, gradually form itself the idea of what the drama was 'about' – its ultimate intellectual, ideological, moral 'meaning'.

The individual signs thus combine into strands or structures, in space as well as time, and these structures in turn re-combine with each other in ever more complex patterns. And these patterns themselves become signifiers of a higher order.

2

Drama as the art form which deploys so many heterogeneous signifiers both in space and time is thus far more hybrid, but also far more complex, than any of the other arts. The visual and acoustic structures it presents are not static and have to be analysed as a series of situations coalescing into movement. It is not only cinema and television drama which can be divided up into a series of 'frames'; a theatrical performance equally consists of a series of 'pictures' containing within themselves a multitude of signifiers that might, if the picture were taken out of the flow, be analysed like those contained in a painting.

What complicates the matter even more is that some of the signifiers in a dramatic performance tend to be present only for a brief moment (i.e. the individual words that make up a passage of dialogue, a gesture or a fleeting facial expression) while others persist for periods of varying length: the set in a stage performance, for example, remains fairly static and allows the spectator, after he has reacted to his first general impression of it, to contemplate and to 'decode' various details in moments of lessened concentration on other aspects of the performance. Thus the spectator might gradually realise the significance of individual items of furniture in a room, the details of the pictures on its wall, which provide clues to the nature, background and history of the characters that inhabit it. The same applies to the costume of the actors or the general colour scheme of the production. In the cinema it is the director who can, after having, for example, established the general appearance of a locality by a long-shot, point the attention of the audience to details within it.

3

Thus, to analyse, understand and 'decode' the multitude of signifiers unleashed by any dramatic performance we must look at them both *synchronically* – i.e. as they function simultaneously at any given moment of the performance – and *diachronically*, as the different types of signifiers coalesce into more complex structures *in time* as the performance proceeds.

At any given instant all the signs deployed contribute to the sum of significance of that single moment in the performance. All these signifiers may pull in the same direction and thus reinforce each other: in a given performance of the storm scene in *King Lear*, say, the picture of swaying trees, the darkness rent by lightning and thunder, the ragged costume and flowing white hair of the king, the dark poetic beauty of his utterance, the huddled figures of his companions, all mutually re-inforce the meaning of that moment in the play.

Or again different signifiers may pull in divergent directions: in the brothel scene in *The Threepenny Opera* the sordidness of the tawdry parlour, the garish costumes of the whores ironise the sentimental tune of the tango that Mac and Jenny are dancing, while the brutal words they sing, in turn, undercut that sentimental melody while, in the corner of the room, the constables are already waiting for Jenny's sign by which she will betray the man to whom she is addressing this 'love'-song. Here the meaning of that moment is constituted by the dialectic of multiple and complex contradictions.

Thus any single moment in a performance can be analysed with a view to understanding the interplay of all the signifiers, iconic, symbolic and deictic, operating within it; or to put it the other way round: the director must decide which signifiers, and what type of interaction between them, to deploy at any given moment in a performance. He will, for example, have to decide whether any, and if so which, signifying system should play the *dominant* role at any given moment; the visuals or the words, the musical or natural sounds, the movement or gestures.

If we look at the structure of signifiers and signifying systems *diachronically*, their inter-action becomes even more complex. Different types of signifiers operate for different segments of time. Some, such as the visual image of the set, the costume or general appearance of leading characters, remain stable throughout a whole scene or act or cinematic sequence, others only make a fleeting appearance.

4

A special place among the signifiers that operate over longer periods of time is occupied by what for a want of a better word one might call 'key' or 'clef' signs. These are signs or signifying elements of a higher order which determine and affect the way the other sign systems within a given section or passage of a work are to be read, and thus act as indicators of the 'level' at which individual signs are to be perceived analogously to the clef signs which determine the clef and key in musical notation.

If, for instance, the opening words of a play are spoken in highly poetic language or verse, this sets the 'key' in which the whole play, or at least that scene, is to be taken by the audience; and while the individual words and sentences are evanescent, the verse-metre or linguistic style of the dialogue may persist through a whole scene, act or, indeed, the entire play. Here, then, the level of language, the metre of the verse, tells the spectators that the intention of the performance is serious and that the action is to be read in a specific way.

For example: there is no verse in everyday communication among people. Hence the use of verse immediately establishes that the play in question will not descend to the level of everyday existence, that the characters and actions displayed in the drama will remain on a given level of abstraction which will exclude certain mundane elements of everyday life and that only the essentials of the situations in the action will be shown, (as in classical French tragedy, where the characters never descend to the level of exchanging polite small talk, eating, or even sitting down). In historical drama, at the same time, the use of verse indicates that no attempt will be made to give a realistic representation of the everyday speech patterns of, say, medieval people.

The choice of vocabulary and metre, moreover, will indicate whether the verse is to be interpreted as a sign that the action is to be viewed at a high level of seriousness; or, say, in a punning and rhyming piece by an author of comic pantomimes like Planché, as outrageous burlesque.

If, as in Shakespeare, there is a transition from blank verse to prose, this signals to the audience that the mood, the 'key' of the action, has changed and that it is shifting onto a more realistic level. The difference between the high poetry of Hamlet's soliloquies (which also signals the lack of realism of such glimpses into the internal thought processes of the hero) and the elegant prose of Hamlet's instructions to the players illustrates the transition to the much more practical and realistic level of the latter, while the low level prose of the gravediggers' banter represents a further descent on the social scale to characters who, as they are deemed not to be capable of higher sentiments, must remain on a level of everyday realism.

These 'key' or 'clef' signs, apart from the all-important one of the level of language include:

- the general colour scheme of a performance;
- the pictorial style of the set, whether realistic or abstract, flat or three-dimensional;
- the cut and period style of the costumes;
- the acting style, whether realistic or grotesque, deeply serious or comedic;
- the mood of the background music, etc.

5

It is on these 'key' or 'clef' signifiers that those highly important and much debated concepts of 'style' and 'genre' are based at the most concrete, 'down-to-earth' level of actual performance.

This, of course, in no way invalidates the venerable traditions of the 'theory of genres', the debate throughout the ages on the nature of tragedy, comedy, tragi-comedy, farce and the other intermediary genres of drama.

These are, essentially 'literary' theories, exploring the nature of situations, their psychological and philosophical aspects as well as the subject matter that is appropriate to the different genres. Insofar as such theories descend to the level of the actual techniques of structuring drama and its performance they have proved extremely vulnerable to the passage of time. The Aristotelian definition of tragedy, for example, so highly valued also by the French neo-classical theorists of the seventeenth century, was shown by the practice of Shakespearean tragedy – and the theoretical writings of critics like Lessing – to be by no means essential to produce the effects – cathartic emotion and an experience of the sublime – that constitute the essence of true tragedy. Similarly the stipulation that tragedy should deal with the fates of persons of high social status and a noble disposition of mind was disproved by, for example, Büchner's *Woyzeck* and the many tragic heroes of his stamp that followed.

The theory of genres, nevertheless, can be shown, in the light of the concept of 'key' or 'clef' signs, to be of great practical importance. By whatever method the director, under modern conditions, decides which genre the play or film he is directing belongs to – be that in the light of his theoretical education or by mere intuition – it will determine his decision by which 'clef' and 'key' signifiers to set the general level on which all the other sign systems will then operate.

Thus the director must arrive at a decision whether he is dealing with a text in the 'clef' or 'key' of tragedy or comedy and then translate this determination of the genre of the performance into concrete terms: whether, to quote one of the most frequently debated examples, one of the major Chekhov plays is to be perceived as mainly comedy or tragedy depends on the level at which the 'key' signifiers are pitched – such as the set, costume, make-up, the degree of seriousness in the acting, the colour and lighting scheme.

Similarly, a text intended to be performed as a tragedy will provoke laughter if the performance with all its 'key' signs is pitched at the wrong level – the play will turn into parody, burlesque or melodrama. It is a cliché, but true nevertheless, that only a hair's breadth separates the sublime from the ridiculous. That dividing line is created, precisely, by the level at which the 'key' signifiers are set from the opening moment of the performance.

Within the major 'clefs' of comedy, tragedy and the other

'genres', there are, of course, further parallel or subsidiary 'keys' determined by the *level* at which such 'key' signifiers are set: these are the basic determinants of the 'style' of the performance. 'Style' depends on the general level of the 'key' signifiers: a combination of all the decisions about which elements are to be used, and which excluded. Which colours, or general colour tonalities (pastel, muted, harsh, glaring, for example), should form the basic mood of the performance, what degree of realism in the acting should be adopted, whether realistic props should be employed, or objects merely suggested by mimed action, etc., and which elements of all these signifying systems must, conversely, be rigidly avoided.

It is through such 'clef' and 'key' signifiers that the audience is made more of the manner in which it is to take the performance. Whether laughter is permitted or desired, or whether to burst out laughing would constitute a 'faux-pas' that might expose the individual's ignorance and lack of social polish.

It will be evident that these 'clef' or 'key' signifiers must depend on the basic assumptions of the society and that their power and effectiveness will depend on the audience's familiarity with the *conventions* under which dramatic performance is practised within a particular culture, or sub-culture. A Western audience might well find Japanese tragedy laughable, or be unable to see the joke in Japanese comedy. We shall return to the problem of dramatic conventions in later chapters.

6

Once the 'clef' and 'key' signifiers have set the general level on which the performance is to be perceived, the individual signs and sign-systems will operate at the differing time-scales of their brief emergence or persistence during the performance.

As the performance unfolds in time the differing signifiers and semiotic systems cohere into developing 'strands', structures with their own progression and rhythm of change: Lear's costume, to remain with our example, will move from royal splendour to raggedness and eventual nudity; the light from sunshine to darkness; the words of the text will form themselves into rhythmic patterns. It is precisely the richness of the detail and the internal cohesion of the individual elements which create the higher and more profound structures of meaning of a dramatic performance.

Each of these discrete structures will in turn mutually affect each other by intertwining in a multitude of contrapuntal and dialectical inter-actions to form a veritable tapestry of intersecting threads, which, in turn, will create the larger clusters of signs that determine the course and content of the performance.

The process by which the signs perceived at any given moment in the performance coalesce into 'strands', and 'structures' or patterns of such strands, throughout the time-span of the performance essentially depends on the operation of the *memory* of the individual spectator. The various detailed 'bits' of information about the time and place of the actions, the names, relationships and moods of the characters, often contradictory and puzzling (like Hamlet's vacillation between violent action and moral scruples), will, insofar as they are kept present in the spectator's short-term memory, finally add up to the perception of a complex personality. The ups-and-downs and complications of the situations and characters, their actions, counter-actions and confrontations, will build into a coherent, if complex, story, fable or plot.

This complex structure of signifiers that constitutes the 'fable' or 'plot' of the drama, which gradually unfolds in the memory and imagination of the spectator, is, in the last analysis, always greater than the sum of its parts.

For the *pace* and *rhythm* of the performance itself becomes one of its major signifiers: the speed at which situations and events succeed each other, the alternation between violent and quiet, or between leisurely and accelerated action – that is: the 'montage' of scenes and sequences both on the stage and on film – give the temporal sequence of action its 'shape', just as the movements of a symphony give form to the amorphous time-element in music.

At this level, 'form' and 'content' are fused to create structure. An action which returns to its starting point like that of *Waiting For Godot* has a different shape from one which relentlessly proceeds in an upward or downward direction: towards the triumph or destruction of the hero, as that of *Oedipus Rex*. These structural patterns of dramatic performance, created by the merging and contrapuntal patterning of the different strands of individual signifiers, moreover, have another vital aspect: monotonous rhythms are dull, because predictable, whereas variety of pace creates surprise, interest and suspense. The rhythm and variety of signifying structures thus determines the way the individual audience member's attention is held, his concentration riveted or relaxed, and thus the way the eventual 'meaning' of the play or film is received.

7

This brings us to the area of dramatic theory and criticism which has been most fully discussed, explored, codified and deconstructed: the nature and basic principles of plot and fable.

An enormous amount has been written about the different types of plot and many of the insights this literature has produced are as valid as ever – always with the caution that most of them are the product of the analysis of different types or styles of drama, and thus only applicable to those particular forms.

If, for a long time in the last century, it was regarded as a general axiom that the plot must relentlessly rise to a climactic moment of reversal before ending with a dying fall, Brecht countered with his demand for a linear succession of self-contained scenes neatly separated from each other to inhibit the audience from being swept away in an emotional trance that would hinder them from thinking critically about the events of the story. Beckett and Ionesco did away with the exposition or with the necessity of a neatly rounded-off ending. And much of contemporary theatrical and cinematic experimentation seeks to dispense with the conventional plot or story-line altogether.

The types of drama that do involve 'narrative' – that is, most of traditional theatre and most cinema and television drama – use the structural forms that are sometimes felt to be the only possible constituents of drama: the opening exposition of the situation; the statement of the basic goal or objective of the action; its gradual complication, twists and turns, until it reaches the turning point or peripeteia at the climax of the drama; and its final unravelling and conclusion.

The most crucial aspect of this type of drama lies in the interrelationship between plot and character: the action will become interesting to the audience only insofar as the characters involved in it arouse the audience's sympathy or emotions, negative as well as positive. Yet because drama is essentially action, the characters in turn can only be developed efficiently by showing them 'in action'. Characters who, in the work of inexperienced playwrights, are merely described by being talked about by other characters remain shadowy. Only what characters *do* tells the audience what they are like. Thus it must be the action of the people within the plot which develops character, while that character of the individuals involved in turn *motivates* the action and makes the plot interesting to follow. Even the most violent events remain uninvolving if they happen to characters the audience does not care about.

8

In the present-day semiological literature the dominant tendencies in looking at plot and character derive from the work of Vladimir Propp, the Russian formalist whose analysis of the structure of the Russian folk-tale classified the characters under seven principal functions (the villain; the donor; the helper; the sought-for person (or 'princess') and her father; the dispatcher; the hero and the false hero)[1], and from Etienne Souriau's

[1] Vladimir Propp, *Morphologie du conte*, Paris: Seuil, 1965.

attempt to create a comprehensive scheme of all possible dramatic situations derived from the permutation and combination of six basic functions in operation within the deep structure of any drama. In his book *Les deux cent mille situations dramatiques*[2] he named these as The Lion (the main thematic drive), The Sun (or representative of Value), The Earth (or the recipient), Mars (or the Opposing force), The Scale (or the Arbiter of the situation) and The Moon (or Helper). By providing each of these functions or forces with astrological symbols Souriau felt he could represent the 'deep structure' of any dramatic text in an algebraic formula. A number of other semioticians (Greimas, Gouhier, Barthes) amended, modified or varied these efforts.

While these attempts at an 'actantional' or 'functional' analysis are ingenious and stimulating, they suffer from the flaw that they are basically reductive. It is difficult to see what illumination or insight can be derived from realising that all dramatic structures are ultimately the same, or merely endless variations on a small number of elements, when in fact their true attraction lies in their almost infinite and wholly unpredictable variety. And, indeed, all attempts to fill existing dramatic works into these schemes lead to not much more than violent and ingenious contortions. We do not need a great deal of theory, for example, to realise that Horatio in *Hamlet* is the hero's 'helper', but what function does Justice Shallow play in the second part of *Henry IV?* And where is the 'princess' in *Endgame?* If we translate the term into that of the 'desired good' (The Sun, Value) of Souriau's scheme, is the princess then the release from earthly existence which may, or may not, be the goal of Hamm's and Clov's endeavours? The moment we begin to apply these schemes, it seems to me, they dissolve into ingenious but useless and misleading games without bringing any deep insights.

[2] Etienne Souriau, *Les deux cent mille situations dramatiques*, Paris: Flammarion, 1950.

Moreover, the critical analysis of plot, character and motivation in drama always tends to be based on the examination of existing successful dramatic texts, and to derive from them normative sets of rules for future work. There is a danger in such pre-ordained patterns, because all rules of this type in the arts tend to lead towards rigidity and fossilisation. The history of drama is full of examples of the deadening effect of such rules derived from critical analysis. One only has to think of the battles between the traditionalists and the Romantics in France, or the obstacles Ibsen or Strindberg had to overcome because they had transgressed age-old rules.

It is of the very essence of true creativity in the arts that it is 'original' and hence outside the pre-ordained established patterns. And while the champions of 'actantional' analysis claim not to want to erect normative rules, their schematic patterns are bound, eventually, to be defeated by the true originality of the genuine innovators who will always find new ways of structuring the action or inaction of drama. Think of Beckett: where is the actantional pattern of a play like *Not I* or *Rockabye*, or a television piece like *Quad?*

9

The action of a dramatic performance will tend to articulate into recognisable segments (acts and scenes, or 'sequences' and 'shots' in the filmic media), and within these into single beats of action or dialogue. Here too repetition, assonance, inversion and variation of the basic elements produces shape – the emergence of form from the flow of action through the time dimension.

Indeed, the combinations and permutations of the different visual, aural and verbal structures that make up the over-all shape of a dramatic performance are infinite. The essential aspect to remember, however, is that drama is process, happening, event, action – and that the imposition of form on such a constantly changing, protean experience depends on articulation: the clear demarcation of distinct parts or phases which can be apprehended as units, as the constituent elements of a larger structure. Hence dramatic structure, analogous to musical structure, depends on the interaction, in sequence, and contrapuntally at any given moment, of melodic and rhythmic elements that are established, varied, juxtaposed, combined and recombined.

This is equally true of the verbal structure and of the visual: in the cinema and in television this is most obvious, but it is equally true of the stage. The dynamics of the stage picture – the grouping of the characters, their sitting down, getting up, entering and leaving the stage – also contain important elements of articulation and renewal, essential for capturing the attention and maintaining the concentration of the audience. The same applies to the sound structure of a dramatic performance. Even in drama with exclusively spoken dialogue it is the variation in tone, pitch, rhythm and pace, usually only subliminally perceived by the audience, that helps to keep them alert rather than lulled by the monotony of the sound pattern. In forms of drama which use music in conjunction with spoken or sung dialogue – film and television drama, melodrama and opera – this function of the underlying sound pattern is even more clear: it is a powerful instrument for the creation of atmosphere, but also for giving form to the temporal structure of the play. In the cinema and in television the use of background music – often hardly perceived by the audience – has become well-nigh indispensable.

It is the rhythmic structure of the different strands of signifiers and the manner in which they form a complex contrapuntal structure very much like that of the orchestral score of a symphony which, in a successful performance, keeps the audience's attention focused, alert and constantly renewed. However fascinating and interesting the action may be on a purely conceptual, intellectual level, without that underlying variety and movement it would inevitably become monotonous and dull and hence the spectator's flagging attention, induced purely physiologically by monotony, would lead them to lose the intellectual thread. The rhythmical structures of interweaving strands of signifiers are the true 'texture' that keeps a dramatic text alive. Their variety, the pattern of their interweaving, functions as one of the main devices that maintain the spectator's desire to arrive at the ultimate 'objective' of the performance and to hold his attention.

These structures thus themselves function as signifying elements by creating the formal patterns that are the basis of the spectator's concentration on the meaning of the performance from moment to moment – suspense.

10

Suspense can be of different kinds: on the most basic level it arises from the question: what will happen next? But it can equally derive from an interest in character, i.e. the question: what will he or she *do*? How will he or she react to the event, the situation?

Or again – and here structure and 'shape' of the performance are of particular signifying force – there is a specific type of suspense created by the formal pattern of the performance itself.

In Beckett's *Waiting For Godot* the meaning of the play emerges only when the audience recognises that the second act has the identical structure as the first. The structure itself acts as a signifier to tell the audience what the play has been saying: namely, that it is a metaphor for the unchanging sameness of human existence, an image of its underlying pattern: the passing of time, experienced as 'waiting', the dependence of human beings on each other, the rhythm of meetings and partings. The suspense of a play in which 'nothing happens' here grows from the gradual unfolding of the image. It is the suspense created when we watch the gradual unfolding of a flower. What holds our attention here is the unfolding, step by step, of a pre-existing pattern. The question in such a dramatic structure is not primarily: what is going to happen next? But simply: what is happening? What image is here being unfolded? This is the structural suspense in plays like those of Genet, Ionesco and Beckett, in the near-abstract 'stage operas' of Robert Wilson, or in films like *L'année dernière à Marienbad*, but, of course, it is also, in attenuated form, present in all dramatic performance, the element which creates the audience's pleasure in the perception of form, the recognition of a circular, a rising or falling underlying formal pattern.

Nor does suspense necessarily depend on surprise or unexpected turns of events. There is also another type of suspense which springs from the recognition of the familiar, the fulfilment of an expectation. It is this which creates the pleasure derived from verse and from rhyme. The most extreme example of this is the peculiar satisfaction derived from viewing a well-known film for the n-th time. The person who goes to see *Casablanca* at every opportunity that presents itself anticipates, from shot to shot, the pleasure of encountering the familiar words, gestures and images. On a lesser level of intensity the stereotyped structures of television series perform a similar function. The viewers of such series are familiar with the pattern. It is the anticipation of the obligatory car-chase or last minute rescue of the hero or heroine at the end of each episode of action series, or of the familiar reactions of the characters in soap opera and situation comedy, and the enjoyment of having these expectations duly fulfilled, with slight variations, which constitutes the pleasure they give to their audiences.

Even in its most frequently encountered form, the anticipation of what is going to happen next, suspense, however, never depends on the totally unexpected. It must always be a subtle combination of the expected with the unexpected. We must know the question before we can become interested in the different possibilities of an answer. In the ritualised pattern of the detective drama, for example, an indefinite number of suspects would diminish rather than excite suspense. It is only when we know that a limited number of characters is under suspicion that our interest in which of them might turn out to be the murderer will produce suspense. Thus the unexpected can only pleasurably arise from the known. That is why at the beginning of any dramatic performance the general ambit of the action, the premise from which it starts, the problem it poses must be clearly stated. Will Hamlet revenge his father's murder? Will Iago succeed in destroying Othello? Will Nora be able to extricate herself from her perilous situation? These are the questions which arouse our expectation and suspense very early in the respective dramatic texts.

Yet upon these main arcs of suspense, which close only at the end of the performance, subsidiary suspense arcs are superimposed. Each scene has its own subsidiary suspense element: at the outset of *Hamlet*, for example, will a ghost appear? It does, but this raises the next suspense element: whose ghost is it? Hamlet recognises it as his father's ghost. What will the ghost tell him? and so on from scene to scene. Each answer to one question contains the elements of another question. That is how the action relentlessly drives forward till the overall, basic question is answered.

Yet within each subsidiary arc of suspense a third, micro-suspense element is superimposed – that is the suspense engendered by the dialectic of the dialogue: each sentence by one character should raise the suspense as to the answer it will receive. Good dialogue is precisely that which never contains a predictable reply (and keep always in mind: the reply need not be verbal, it might be a gesture, the raising of an eyebrow). On the minutest scale this is summed up in the basic truth about acting: that its ultimate secret lies in *timing*, that is, the shaping of each sentence into a pattern with the maximum content of suspense and surprise. It is that pause of a fraction of a second before the decisive word in the sentence, that produces the frisson or the laughter. Parallel to the suspense element in the unfolding of the action, runs the element of character suspense: each action of a character, each word he or she utters, adds another piece of circumstantial evidence to the revelation of his or her true nature.

II

A dramatic performance, whether on stage or screen, thus is a complex texture of individual signifiers as well as strands and clusters of signifiers, emerging in a rich profusion of rhythmical, visual, melodic and tonal patterns. A dramatic performance is a 'text' infinitely richer, more multi-layered than a literary text and hence open to a much larger number of possible interpretations by its recipients.

Insofar as a dramatic performance is based on a written – not necessarily 'literary' – text (it could also be a choreographic notation, a scenario for improvisation, the story-line of a mime-play), that text passes through two distinct phases of 'reading' or 'de-coding' or 'interpretation'.

The first 'reading' is that of the individual – or collective of individuals – who will be responsible for the performance of the text. They – the director, the designers of sets and costumes, the musician, lighting designer, maker of properties etc., or, in the cinema, the artists responsible for deciding on the camera angles, viewpoints, close-ups, editing and pacing of sequences, etc. – must arrive at decisions about the 'meaning' of the written text which exclude many other possible 'readings'.

For example: they will have to decide whether to put *Hamlet* into medieval, Renaissance or perhaps contemporary dress, whether to concentrate on the revenge-theme or the philosophical and psychological interpretations of the action, and on a multitude of other variable readings of the well-nigh infinite number of implications the original text carries with it. And to crown it all, each line, each syllable of the text, each gesture, each raising of the eyebrows of each character implies a further 'interpretation'.

But this first interpretative reading of the text in turn becomes, at the second stage, the basic 'text' for each individual spectator, who now has to 'read' and 'interpret' the 'performance text', which again is open to a further infinite number of 'readings' and 'interpretations' within the parameters that have been drawn by the performers' reading of the original blueprint they have interpreted.

It is here that the simplified model of the 'theory of communication' has to be seen in its true proportion of applicability. A simple factual message: 'arriving 3.30 pm' has a single, clear 'meaning'. A sentence in a literary text, a poem or novel, will have a much larger number of overtones and associations, but it will still clearly be emanating from a well-defined source, sender or author, and be open to multiple interpretations, yet only within fairly well defined parameters.

The same 'message' – i.e. the same words – put onto stage or screen has undergone a sea-change. Now these words have already undergone a process of 'interpretation' and are now radiating, as it were, diffused through a prism which disperses the single message into a spectrum of different colours: the person who speaks the words, his appearance, his gestures, his intonations, the visual environment in which he speaks the words, and a multitude of other factors have been introduced and offer the recipient of the message a multitude of possible points upon which he can concentrate his attention.

This, then, is the basic paradox of dramatic performance: the richness, the multi-layered 'thickness' of the texture of what is presented to the recipients of the communication infinitely enhances its complexity and expressive potential, while at the same time rendering it much more difficult to concentrate on any specific 'message' or even to focus the recipients' attention to any specific area or aspect of the utterance – whether that be a 'message' or whatever else it may communicate.

Indeed can we still speak of a 'message' when even the identity of the 'sender' of the communication has become somewhat problematic? *Who* exactly is it who has interpreted the blueprint of the performance, the original verbal text? That, in itself, is by no means clear, a question to which there can be a conclusive answer. True, nowadays it is assumed that it is, ultimately, the 'director', 'metteur-en-scène', 'Regisseur', or as the Scandinavian languages put it very graphically 'Instructeur' (i.e. the teacher who tells the other executants how to read the text and what to do with it). But that is merely a convenient way of putting the responsibility for what is essentially a collective creation by many individuals onto one individual who puts his signature to it.

There are very few directors – on stage or screen – whose personality and creative potential is strong enough really to become the origin and source of *everything* that has signifying force within a performance. And even such a major director can merely determine and prescribe the main objectives of the communication that is to take place, but must still, necessarily, rely on the input of a multitude of other creative individuals, each of whom retains a considerable amount of autonomy within his own field. And, ultimately, certainly in a live performance, but also in the cinema and on television, it is the *actors* who stand in the front-line of the performance, on whose responses, inflections, gestures, appearance and charisma the communication ultimately depends.

Thus a dramatic performance consists of a large number of 'messages' emanating from a number of 'senders' and consisting of a multitude of individual signs, signifiers, and signifying structures. These may ultimately, for the individual spectator, cohere into a 'message' or convey 'meaning' on a variety of levels, but, as it is difficult to locate a single source of that 'message' or 'meaning', it would be more accurate to speak of a dramatic performance not as a single 'act of communication' of a 'message', but rather as of an *'event'* witnessed by the spectators.

And, indeed, this tallies with, and emerges from, the very

nature of drama: if drama is 'mimetic action' recreating real or imaginary events – conflicts, battles, interactions, fantasies, dreams as they occur in 'life' – what else can those mimetic recreations be but, in their turn, 'events' as multivalent as the events we confront in our 'real' life. That these events have meaning is beyond doubt, but those meanings are elusive, open to interpretation, and impossible to pin down.

Indeed, art condenses, clarifies, orders and enhances in its mimesis what is chaotic, amorphous, murky and inconsequential in 'reality'. But drama, as the most complex and complete mimesis of reality must, necessarily, still retain that element of multivalence of the event itself. The absence of a clearly defined individual source of the communication, moreover, makes it impossible to provide, within the performance, an authoritative commentary or interpretation of the action, such as, for example, a novelist, speaking in his own persona, can supply by expressing his own opinion of the events he portrays. There is no authorial voice in drama, nor can there be, ultimately, a clear and univocal 'directorial' voice, not even in the cinema, where 'auteur theories' have long since been a staple of critical theorising. Even the films of Chaplin, who wrote, directed, composed and acted his own films are, however, open to multiple interpretations, and cannot be reduced to a single 'message' he, Chaplin intended, because, for example, some of the actors or technicians involved may not have quite accurately followed his instructions. A dramatic performance of any kind must be a complcx 'event' that cannot be reduced to the utterance of a single voice, as a novel can, which, though it may also be open to complex, multivalent interpretations can at least be regarded as, at least on the conscious plane, the willed utterance of a single author.

All this, of course, is not to say that definite strands or layers of meaning cannot be clearly understood and de-coded by the spectators. On the level of pure denotation the different strands of signifiers in, say, *Hamlet*, will undoubtedly achieve a clear consensus that Hamlet had been given the task to avenge his father's murder, that he hesitated and ultimately achieved his objective at the cost of his own life. In the same way, in 'real' life there will be a consensus that, say, a car accident has happened to a friend. What will still remain open will be the ultimate 'meaning', the significance of such an event. And the same applies, if more intensively, to the dramatic event of *Hamlet.*

For here the director and his co-artists will have endeavoured to structure the performance towards imparting something of an interpretation of the chain of actions that constitute the play. Nevertheless, there will still be an immense divergence of individual interpretations and meanings of this distilled, clarified, ordered mimesis of real life.

The ultimate meaning of the dramatic event will depend on each individual spectator's own 'reading' of its complex 'performance text'.

XII

The Performers and the Audience

I

A veritable cornucopia of signs and the 'message' each of them is intended to convey – or conveys unintentionally – is unloaded upon the audiences of a dramatic performance. The individual signs, as we have seen, will tend to coalesce into larger structures of signification. Yet what the performance will ultimately be 'saying' to its audience, what it will 'mean' to each member of that collective entity, will in turn depend on each individual spectator's capacity or 'competence' to understand or 'decode' the individual signs and sign structures, as well as his or her readiness to devote sufficient attention to it to 'take it all in'. (In the 'age of television' this has become more crucial than ever.)

From this it follows that the ultimate 'meaning' – that is the residue of the 'message' or 'content' of the performance which emerges in the spectator's mind while the performance unfolds and remains in his memory after it ends – must be different for each individual member of the audience.

This total picture should, as we have seen, rest on the basis of a more or less generally shared *consensus* on what happened to whom in the drama. Even so, there will always be some in the audience who just 'did not get' even that much. Such oft-repeated anecdotes as that about the old ladies walking out of Ibsen's *Ghosts*, remarking, 'Well, I suppose the poor boy had consumption', do have a foundation in fact; similarly uncomprehending spectators can be found at the end of any performance.

Such confusions and misinterpretations arise from two distinct sources: either a lack of 'competence' to understand what is going on: in the case of *Ghosts* an ignorance of the existence or problems of venereal disease or at least, provided the performance was a competent one, of the euphemisms by which alone it could be hinted at in Victorian society; or a lack of interest, attention and concentration.

Drama builds its representation of reality in a non-linear, non-systematic manner: the spectator has to be alert to pick up the basic elements of the 'exposition' and the subsequent concatenation of events, and to integrate them into a total picture. If the attention flags or is distracted, an essential link in the chain may be missed and the whole structure fails to cohere, to 'make sense'. This may sometimes be the fault of the performance itself. If two characters, for example, are played by actors who look too much alike, it may be difficult for some spectators to tell them apart; important facts may not emerge clearly enough from the dialogue. But most frequently it results from the audience's lack of interest and concentration, which, in turn, is also often due to weaknesses in the story-line or direction. It simply was not 'gripping' enough, 'did not hold the attention'.

The audience's attentiveness and concentration – and, indeed, its very presence in the theatre, cinema or in front of the television set – in turn depends on its preliminary estimate of the potential interest of what is being offered. This is the function of the preliminary and framing signifiers: they create the level of expectation which draws the audience to the performance in the first place and sets the pitch of its initial mood and readiness to receive what is being offered. This, in turn, leads to an even more fundamental question; what motivates the performers to offer, and the audience to want to experience, the performance?

2

The class of activities into which drama falls is almost automatically assumed by scholars and critics (myself among these) to be that of 'Art'. But leaving aside the thorny question of how art itself is to be defined, clearly drama can also be classed under other headings.

For example, drama, in our world, is a business, an industry. By most of its consumers it is regarded as an entertainment, a way to pass the time, to be taken out of oneself, to be diverted, distracted. Drama can also be considered as a 'cultural phenomenon': a ritual by which a society communes with itself, even a quasi-religious activity. As such it is to be taken with the utmost seriousness; in some countries their 'national' theatres are veritable shrines in which the national identity is daily celebrated.

Yet drama is also a 'ludic' activity springing from sheer playfulness or the fun of impersonation; children playing fathers and mothers, or doctors and patients, are engaging in improvised drama, both as a form of pleasurable, joyful self-expression and also as a learning process. And Brecht, in formulating his Lehrstück-theory, even postulated drama of this type, without an audience, as a way in which the actors themselves could learn about the world, about how the victim as well as the executioner felt, by playing these parts in turn. Here the players themselves form their own audience.

All this raises the question: what the fundamental aspect of drama might be that underlies all these very diverse and divergent objectives and motivations for which dramatic representation is undertaken? What is the one basic incentive for drama, which will allow us to understand the essential method of its working, through which it meets all these seemingly so different needs, purposes, demands and requirements?

What, to start with, we must ask, motivates the audience? Why do people want to experience drama, why should they, as Hamlet says, sit at a play and expose themselves to the 'very cunning of the scene'?

Shakespeare (who clearly knew more about drama than most practitioners of the art – or business?) provides what I feel is the simplest, most fundamental motivation for all audiences: in *A Midsummer Night's Dream* Theseus, the Duke of Athens, on his wedding-evening calls for a play:

> To wear away this long age of three hours
> Between our after-supper and bed-time?
> ....
> What revels are in hand? Is there no play
> To ease the anguish of a torturing hour?
> ....How shall we beguile
> The lazy time, if not with some delight. (V.I)

The motivation of the audience here is simply the need to pass the time pleasurably. That expectation of some pleasure or delight, of aesthetic gratification, surely underlies all the other motivations which bring an audience to a dramatic performance. This is the bedrock on which must rest all the higher gratifications that drama can bring, the basic objective that induces human beings to expose themselves to a dramatic performance. The need to fulfil that expectation of a time pleasurably passed *must* be the basic structural principle behind *all* dramatic performance, even that which, ultimately, aims at higher levels of experience (emotional, intellectual, didactic, sublimely cathartic, religious or quasi-religious).

Hamlet could not have caught Claudius' conscience had not the expectation of a diverting experience lured the king to attend that presentation of 'The Mousetrap'.

This basic truth is also acknowledged by another great practitioner of drama, Bertolt Brecht – the same who had at the start of his career thought of drama as a didactic tool, a teaching instrument that might not need even spectators as long as the actors themselves learned something from the activity of role-playing. Twenty years after insisting on the purely didactic purpose of drama, he had totally changed his mind. In his *Little Organon For The Theatre* he starts with the following definition:

> Theatre consists in producing living images of traditional or fictional events among human beings – for entertainment.[1]

And he stresses:

> It has always been the business of theatre – as of all the other arts – to entertain people. This business gives it its special dignity; it needs no other justification than being fun (Spass) – but that justification it *must* have. It would be impossible to raise it to a higher status by, for instance, turning it into a market for morals; it would rather, in that case, have to make sure that it should thereby not be lowered in status, which would immediately happen, if it did not make morality enjoyable, enjoyable for the senses – by which, incidentally, morality could only profit.[2]

Brecht does not deny the religious, ritual origins of drama:

> If it is said that theatre originated from ritual, what is said is merely that it became theatre by leaving the ritual sphere; what it took from the mysteries was not their ritual purpose but their pleasurableness, pure and simple. And that catharsis of Aristotle, that purging by fear and pity, or of fear and pity, is a cleansing which was carried out not only in a pleasurable manner, but basically for the express purpose of enjoyment.[3]

But, Brecht adds, there are

> .... weak (simple) and strong (complex) types of entertainment which theatre can produce. The latter, which we encounter in great dramatic works, achieve their intensi-

[1] Brecht, *Kleines Organon für das Theater* in *Gesammelte Werke* vol VII, Frankfurt: Suhrkamp, 1967, p. 663.
[2] ibid. p. 663/4.
[3] ibid. p. 664.

> fication in the same way in which, for example copulation is enhanced by love; these [more complex, stronger, higher level] sources of entertainment are multi-layered, richer in internal correspondences, more contradictory and have more far-reaching, lasting effects.[4]

It is the desire for, and expectation of, these various forms of simple and complex gratification that brings audiences to drama. As regards the motivation of the performers: here too *A Midsummer Night's Dream* provides some insights.

When it looks as though the rude mechanicals have lost the chance of putting on their play because of the absence of the leading member of the cast, Snug, the joiner, and Flute, the bellows-mender, let the cat out of the bag:

> If our sport had gone forward, we had all been made men.
>
> O sweet bully Bottom! Thus hath he lost sixpence a day during his life; he could not have scap'd sixpence a day. (IV.2)

Sixpence a day for life amounted to a considerable income in Shakespeare's England. The rude mechanicals were after a fortune to be bestowed upon them by the Duke's bounty in recognition of their efforts to entertain him.

So much for the motives of the players in this case. But, of course, financial gain is not the only motivation for dramatic performance, although in our own time, it is the principal one. Hamlet wants to catch the conscience of the king by his staging of the Murder of Gonzago: thus the release of deep emotion and profound insights (whether religious experience, moral uplift, political propaganda, or indeed, the arousing of feelings of guilt) can be, frequently has been and still often is, an important objective of dramatic performance. Although the rude mechanicals are motivated by the desire to achieve a substantial annuity, their performance of 'The most lamentable

[4] ibid. p. 664/5.

comedy and most cruel death of Pyramus and Thisbe' is obviously also intended (in pursuit of that primary objective) to be a true work of art, a true tragedy, as such designed to purge the emotions of its audience by fear and pity. Yet, ironically, it achieves notable success in the very opposite manner – as a source of great mirth for the sophisticated spectators.

The message that reaches its recipients is thus vastly different from what the senders of the message intended. When Hippolyta declares:

> This is the silliest stuff that I ever heard.

Theseus retorts:

> The best in this kind are but shadows; and the worst are no worse, if imagination amend them.

Hippolyta replies:

> It must be your imagination then, and not theirs. (V.1)

Thus it is the spectator's imagination that produces the final effect, the ultimate meaning, if indeed meaning is to be the end of the experience, rather than mere idle entertainment.

A Midsummer Night's Dream, however, is 'metadrama' (i.e. drama within and about drama) of high complexity: for in the rude mechanicals' play one of the main concerns of the performers is, at all costs, to avoid *offending* their audience. Explanatory prologues and cautionary addresses to the audience are variously inserted in the tragedy during the rehearsals we witness, in order to minimise the horror or distaste the ladies might experience, for example, when a roaring lion appears. Shakespeare, the master communicator, is mocking not only the incompetence of these amateur actors, but also their pathetic anxiety to *please* rather than to shock or offend their audience.

But then Shakespeare himself, in his own play's epilogue, resorts to exactly the same device of trying to pacify his audience (probably, just like the courtly audience in Theseus' palace in the play, high-born lords and ladies trying to divert themselves on the evening of a solemn wedding) by an almost identical resort to direct apology in Puck's epilogue:

> If we shadows have offended
> Think but this, and all is mended,
> That you have but slumbered here
> While these visions did appear.
> And this weak and idle theme
> No more yielding but a dream.
> Gentles, do not reprehend.
> If you pardon, we will mend.

Anxiety to please their audience, not to offend it so that the reward of their efforts is secured, here appears as at least one of the motivations, not only of the ridiculous clowns of the play within the play, but equally that of Shakespeare and his actors; he also accepts that to pass the time pleasurably, to while away an idle hour, without being unduly frightened or offended, is the main motive that draws an audience to drama.

As the great Dr Johnson put it most concisely in the prologue he wrote for Garrick at the Drury Lane Theatre:

> For we that live to please, must please to live.

It would be quite wrong, however, to interpret this last statement as an affirmation of mere greed for the spectators' money or approbation. That a deep need for self-expression, an imperious creative urge inspires many of the artists – writers, actors, directors, designers – involved in drama is beyond doubt. It is precisely the tension between the need for self-expression and the need to 'please', to 'reach' an audience that constitutes the basic dialectics of performance. Excessive pandering to the audience's known preferences, a deliberate exploitation of proven formulas produces the repetitive regurgitation of proven past successes which, because it becomes predictable and uninteresting, ultimately defeats that very end of giving pleasure through novelty and the unexpected; excessive concentration on self-expression without regard to the audience's needs leads to self-indulgent work which, in extreme cases, will fail to communicate and remain totally obscure and solipsistic.

The expression of the deepest creative urges, therefore, can only take place if the audience's basic need for comprehension and the resulting aesthetic gratification (pleasure, laughter, cathartic uplift) is met. Only if the prospect of such gratification remains constantly before them will the spectators be ready and able to summon up the concentration and attentiveness that will render them capable of creating out of the plethora of individual signs they receive the imaginary structure that in their minds will constitute the 'message' or 'meaning' of the performance they have witnessed.

It is to achieve that primary objective that all the sign systems at the disposal of dramatic performance must be deployed and structured.

Ultimately this means that a dramatic performance can be seen – to enlarge our initial definition – as a sequence of representations, images, illustrations of human life by human beings *designed in such a way that they will evoke the maximum of preliminary interest* – so that spectators will make the decision and effort to come and watch them – *and then to capture and hold their attention and concentration* so efficiently that they will follow the dramatic event with delight to the point of forgetting their own concerns of the moment, as well as conquering momentarily the boredom which accompanies so much of our waking life.

The success of any dramatic performance thus depends on its ability to arouse interest and expectations which it can keep alive by holding the spectator's attention until their final fulfilment – or, in other words, by creating continued suspense, that is, the desire to keep watching for what is going to happen next.

A dramatic performance must, thus, basically, at the most

elementary level, be regarded as an event designed to *capture* and *hold* the attention of those for whom it is intended. All other conceptual and emotional effects of such a performance depend on the fulfilment of that basic premise.

Here, then, we come down to the psychological and physiological bedrock of the aesthetics of dramatic performance: the state of concentration and attention of the audience. As another great dramatist who also was a highly experienced practitioner, Goethe, puts it in the 'Prologue on the Theatre' to *Faust*, the performers have to overcome formidable initial obstacles:

Wenn diesen Langeweile treibt
Kommt jener satt vom übertischten Mahle
Und was das allerschlimmste bleibt
Gar mancher kommt vom Lesen der Journale.
Man eilt zerstreut zu uns wie zu den Maskenfesten,
Und Neugier nur beflügelt jeden Schritt
Die Damen geben sich und ihren Putz zum besten
Und spielen ohne Gage mit. . . .

[If this one is driven by boredom,
that one comes satiated from an overfull table
and what is worst of all
many come from reading the journals.
They come to us absentmindedly
Curiosity alone motivates their steps
The ladies display themselves and their finery
and play their part without being paid for it.]

And what is worse, many of the spectators are merely filling in the time until the next pleasures they anticipate:

Der, nach dem Schauspiel hofft ein Kartenspiel
Der eine wilde Nacht an einer Dirne Busen!
Was plagt ihr armen Toren viel
Zu solchem Zweck die holden Musen?[5]

[5] Goethe, *Faust, Eine Tragödie*, 'Vorspiel auf dem Theater', lines 13–19 and 24–27.

> [This one, after the play hopes for a game of cards,
> That one for a wild night on a whore's bosom!
> Why should you, poor fools,
> plague the lovely Muses to such ends?]

It is against these handicaps that the performers have to fight to evoke attention and concentration. The degree of that concentrated – or diffuse, attentuated – attention is something one can sense, even measure. Certainly the performers in a theatre can feel it: in the silence of the audience or in their reaction in laughter or held breath, if their attention is being engaged; in their restlessness, coughing and whispering, if it is not. In the case of television the effort to achieve attention in the familiar environment of the home with all its distractions is even greater.

The attention span of individuals and crowds is limited, too long a wait for the fulfilment of an expectation makes the attention flag; hence, as we have seen, the structure of a dramatic event in the dimension of time must follow a dialectic of constantly aroused new expectation, which, once fulfilled gives rise to further, new ones. Hence the articulation of dramatic events into the patterned structures in time, discussed in the previous chapter: visual, conceptual, actional, and aural.

Monotony is deadly to all the senses, it deadens the attention even to the point of putting it to sleep. Hence even on the purely physiological level the structural principle underlying all these patterns must be that of constant movement, the creation of variety, change, surprise.

How to hold the attention and to rivet the concentration of their audience, that is the ultimate skill the creators of a dramatic performance must master.

XIII

The Audience's Competence: Social Conventions and Personal Meanings

I

The skill of the creators of any dramatic performance in issuing and weaving together their multifarious structures of signs can have its impact only if the spectators exposed to them know what they stand for. As one of the world's leading experts on 'oral literature' (of which dramatic performance clearly is an instance) puts it:

> (A text) . . . can be made into an utterance only by a code that is existing and functioning in a living person's mind.[1]

Thus the skill of the creators of the performance must be matched by, and depends on, the 'competence' of the spectators to 'decode' if not all at least a sufficient minimum of the signs and sign systems deployed within the performance.

The overwhelming majority of all the signs used in daily life as well as in the arts, however, is far from universally valid or comprehensible. We may know what a person's type of dress or haircut indicates because we are familiar with the dress code of our civilisation. We understand what he says because we know the language he uses. We are impressed or disgusted by his behaviour because we know the code of good manners in our particular society, culture, or sub-culture. If the person concerned comes from a different society, we might well fail to

[1] Walter J. Ong, 'Text as Interpretation' in *Oral Tradition in Literature* (ed. J. M. Foley), Columbia: University of Missouri Press, 1986, pp. 148–9.

understand or misinterpret the signs he carries in his dress, hairstyle and manners, and we shall fail to understand his language, unless we have learned its code. Most of the signs we use actively or perceive passively in our daily lives are 'culturally determined'.

Only very few gestures or facial expressions might be described as being instantly understood by all human beings, regardless of their cultural or social background: perhaps such deictic gestures as pointing with the finger, or the screams of instinctive, spontaneous fear and terror, or the distorted features produced by rage.

Even the mere physical appearance of an actor or actress is not without its culturally determined significance: what is beauty in one culture or at one epoch does not necessarily conform to the ideals of another culture, or another epoch. In some cultures the fatter a woman is, the more beautiful she is considered, in our present Western culture, slimness is regarded as the height of attractiveness. In the cinema actresses once adored as the glamorous beauties of fifty years ago tend now to appear far less attractive, or even downright dowdy and ridiculous, as our own divas will no doubt to future generations. The non-verbal signs understood and used within a society, culture or sub-culture are thus as much specific to their locality and epoch as verbal languages. Not only has each nationality or ethnic group its own language, there are also the innumerable variations in regional dialect and idiom, in specialised languages of different professions or social groups, as well as the variations all these languages undergo through time. A play using the professional jargon of agronomists or computer engineers may well contain much that will be incomprehensible to spectators of the same language group unfamiliar with these specialised idioms. And similarly the plays of Shakespeare contain many verbal signifiers that will be lost on most ordinary English-speakers today.

Thus the ability of the individual spectator of a play, film or television performance to take in what he is being shown will vary according to his or her 'competence', his or her familiarity with the mores, implicit assumptions and language of the fictional world he is being exposed to. He must know the 'conventions', linguistic and behavioural of that world.

In addition he or she will have to be familiar with the techniques by which this world is being represented in drama. Thus he or she must also know at least the basis of the dramatic or cinematic 'conventions' of the specific dramatic medium.

Thence the 'conventions' shaping a performance and challenging the individual spectator's 'competence' to understand and 'decode' the signs presented to her or him, can be seen to fall into two distinct categories:

> – conventions of the particular culture, civilisation or society to which performers and spectators belong: *cultural, behavioural or ideological conventions.*

and

> – conventions governing the presentation of the dramatic performance: *dramatic or performance conventions.*

2

The general cultural conventions which are iconically represented in the performance cover the entire scope of life and behaviour within that culture, its language, manners, moral standards, rituals, tastes, ideologies, sense of humour, superstitions, religious beliefs, the entire body of its store of ideas and concepts.

It is clear that not all spectators, even within the same cultural sphere, will be equally familiar with all aspects of all the conventions that are involved: for example, an eighteenth-century agricultural labourer might well have missed some of the finer points of manners and aristocratic mores on which an understanding of the wit of a Restoration comedy by Congreve or Vanbrugh depended, nor would his vocabulary have been large enough to follow much of the refined language of the dialogue. There is a need for competence in specific 'subcultural conventions' to arrive at a full understanding of a dramatic performance text.

These may derive from the finer points of manners and behaviour in specific social milieus or a knowledge of the connotations of the meaning of certain words, in particular proper names. The mention by the tramp Davies in Pinter's *The Caretaker* that his personal documents are being held for him in Sidcup evokes hilarity in a London audience, simply because the name of that particular suburb suggests certain associations of lower-middle class semi-detached houses that are the very antithesis of a repository of official documents. Similarly, even the numbers of different New York streets – at first sight the most clinically sterile type of label – carry a wealth of connotations for those familiar with 42nd or 8th Street. Much of the humour of situation comedy on television depends on a knowledge of the life-style and behaviour patterns of the respective middle or lower-middle class sub-cultures.

For a certain number of audience members, moreover, depending on their previous experience and sophistication, the meaning of a given performance will be influenced by a variety of other factors, such as items of information or knowledge inherent in the general cultural milieu of their particular society, culture or sub-culture. Such, for one, are the more or less subtle undercurrents of meaning arising from 'intertextuality': references to, parallels with, or variations on matters presumed to be 'generally known' in that milieu. The 'myths' and stories that shape the popular consciousness fall under this heading.

In the context of present-day popular drama this is one of the basic sources for the audience's understanding and enjoyment of the innumerable series and serials on television: here the fore-knowledge of the personalities and behavioural idiosyncrasies of the leading characters (and their performers) and an awareness of the very strongly established pattern of the structure on which each episode is based not only makes these dramatic episodes easier to follow but produces meaning through the very variations of the structural pattern that each episode brings. The immense popularity of drama using stereotyped characters and highly formalised structures of plot – from the Greek New Comedy through the Italian *commedia dell'arte* to present day television series – springs from this source of expectation and delight: the additional meaning derived from previous knowledge of the material and its implications.

And what is true of the shallow delights of popular entertainment is equally so when we think of the highest reaches of drama. The use of a relatively narrow range of plots taken from myth in ancient Greek tragedy also relied on the individual spectator's familiarity with the characters and plot-lines (which were part of the culture itself and thus belonged to the realm of cultural or sub-cultural convention) and his delight in the brilliance and wit with which these basic 'givens' were subtly varied, parodied or subverted by individual authors. And this process has continued throughout Western cultural history – at least for those spectators who remained familiar with Greek culture. The meaning of, say, Jean Anouilh's *Antigone* derives for such people from their knowledge of the play by Sophocles on the same theme, a comparison of the two and the intellectual delight in recognising the subtle variations and re-valuations of the familiar events and concepts by the modern author. One could argue that a considerable amount of the meaning of most dramatic experiences derives from such previous intertextual knowledge. And here again 'text' does not merely denote the verbal element of the drama but the entire 'texture' of interacting sign systems: gestures, visual patterns, in the cinema 'quotation' of classical models of mise-en-scène, camera angles and editing, also carry the same subtle undercurrents of nostalgic, parodistic or dialectical significance.

3

Equally important as familiarity with the totality of the cultural conventions of the society in question for an understanding of the meaning of a dramatic performance is an awareness of the specific dramatic or performance conventions within that culture, society or subculture, as well as those of the specific dramatic medium or sub-genre: stage-play (e.g. tragedy, comedy, farce), opera, cabaret, cinema (e.g. Western, musical, thriller), television (e.g. situation comedy, police-serial), etc.

These in turn can be seen as falling into two separate categories: the basic assumptions underlying dramatic performance in general, which tend to be the same in different cultures: such as the audience's need to be aware that the events shown are fictional rather than real; that people who are killed are not really dead; that the actors' personalities are not identical with those of the characters; that the fictional world of the stage or screen continues beyond its frame, etc. (The old anecdote about the yokel who, as Kean cried: 'My kingdom for a horse!', shouted from the auditorium: 'Will an ass do?', to which Kean retorted: 'Yes, sir, step right up onto the boards!', illustrates what happens if these basic conventions are unknown to an individual.) And, secondly: the specific and extremely varied conventions that govern specific varieties, genres and subgenres of dramatic performance.

These conventions are well-nigh infinite in variety. Some, like those governing the performance of classical Greek tragedy, Japanese traditional drama (Noh, Kiyogen, Kabuki) or Chinese classical theatre, are highly formalised and rigid. Other forms of drama allow a certain amount of flexibility and create new conventions from case to case as they develop.

Thus, to mention just some of the best-known instances, the audiences of ancient Greek drama had a certain pre-conception of what a theatre looked like (they would have been baffled by curtains, artificial lighting etc.); they expected that the actors had to be masked, that there were choral passages that had a certain function and meaning, and that the formal structure of dialogic and choric scenes followed a rigid pre-set pattern.

In traditional Japanese theatre, stage hands dressed in black who intervene in the action are deemed to be invisible. In Chinese classical opera a performer with a flag represents a whole army.

The audiences of medieval mystery plays had to know that the characters emerging from one of the several mansions upon the stage were supposed to be in the environment represented by that mansion even when distant from it.

The spectators in the Elizabethan playhouse could 'read' the meaning of scenes performed 'within', on the inner stage, or 'above' on the raised part of the stage; and nineteenth-century audiences knew that they were looking into, say, a room 'through' a transparent fourth wall; and similarly present-day audiences in the cinema and television understand the meanings of 'fades', 'dissolves' and changing camera-angles.

In the European theatre for centuries 'asides' spoken by one of the characters to the audience were deemed to be inaudible to other performers on stage; characters who were visible to the audience and must have been so to other performers were deemed to be invisible to them, simply because they were supposed to be hidden by the trunk of a slim tree or a rudimentary screen; characters identically dressed were accepted as looking completely indistinguishable and could thus be mistaken for each other, although the joke for the audience resided precisely in their being aware which twin was being mistaken for the other; in the Western film it was conventional that the villain should wear black, the hero light costumes. . . . The list could be prolonged almost indefinitely.

It is characteristic of our own Western civilisation that, through the immense increase in the availability of drama, it has become so eclectic that audiences have become familiar with a multitude of different dramatic conventions and sub-conventions. Most individuals in the Western world can read the performance conventions of cinema, television drama, and a multitude of stage conventions: peep-show, arena, 'in–the round', street-theatre and a variety of others. The same is true of the numerous sub-conventions governing the understanding of different genres, sub-genres and performance styles: musical comedy, opera, the thriller, tragedy, comedy, farce, to name but a few of the more obvious theatrical ones; and of the various 'genres' of the cinema (the Western, science fiction, slapstick, domestic drama etc., etc.) and television, with its specific conventions for series, mini-series, serials, soap opera, situation comedy, etc., etc.

Each of these genres sets up a specific expectation, a specific adjustment to thematic, structural and stylistic assumptions underlying the particular convention in those audience members that are familiar with them.

4

The vast expansion of the availability of dramatic performance and the rise of an eclectic approach to past forms of drama in the wake of the rise of the consciousness of historical change in the course of the nineteenth century has led to a veritable proliferation of different dramatic conventions in present-day Western civilisation.

This has led to a fragmentation of the audience into various sub-groups, characterised by the different degrees of familiarity with different dramatic conventions which they might be deemed to bring to a performance. The people who attended Peter Hall's *Oresteia* in the British National Theatre, performed in masks by an all-male cast, were assumed to know something about the background and convention of Greek drama that was being reconstructed (though only partially: why were there masks but no cothurni?). The audiences who flock to Oberammergau are deemed to know something about the religious mystery play tradition of Central Europe.

Of course, an intelligent spectator can pick up at least some of the ground-rules of an unfamiliar convention as he goes along. The persistent innovative drive and desire to break new and original ground which is so characteristic of modern Western culture also leads to a constant change in the conventions of dramatic performance. The history of theatrical scandals accompanying the introduction of such innovations from the 'Battle of Hernani' in 1831 to the scandals caused by Ibsen, Wagner or Beckett illustrates the process by which such new conventions are established. A section of the audience nurtured in the old convention may completely fail to understand such a performance, while others 'decode' the new convention as it unfolds.

To quote just one example: Ibsen did not only scandalise the audiences of the 1880s by the unusual and daring nature of his subject matter. Although he adhered fairly strictly to the convention of the nineteenth-century 'well-made play', his desire to be more realistic led him to the virtual abandonment of the 'aside'. This was, in some ways, even more bewildering to the audience than mentions of venereal disease or women's rights. One of the leading, and extremely intelligent, London critics, Clement Scott, as late as 1891, declared himself baffled by a performance of *Rosmersholm*:

> The old theory of playwriting was to make your story or your study as simple and direct as possible. The hitherto accepted plan of a writer for the stage was to leave no possible shadow of a doubt concerning his characterisation. But Ibsen loves to mystify. He is as enigmatical as the Sphinx. Those who earnestly desire to do him justice and to understand him keep on saying to themselves: 'Granted these people are egotists, or atheists, or agnostics, or emancipated, or whatnot, still I can't understand why he does this or she does that.'[2]

[2] Clement Scott, unsigned review in the *Daily Telegraph*, 24 February 1891, quoted from Michael Egan (ed.) *Ibsen, the Critical Heritage*, London and Boston: Routledge and Kegan Paul, 1972, p. 168.

The need, created by the new naturalistic convention, to *deduce* the characters' inner thoughts – the 'subtext' – had not yet been recognised by an audience member like Clement Scott, nor the skill required to 'decode' the subtext through a very concentrated observation of their seemingly trivial surface behaviour been learned. Today, when the more sophisticated theatre-goer has acquired that skill, Ibsen's plays, if anything, suffer from being too transparent and over-explicit about the characters' feelings.

Moreover, beyond the generic or stylistic conventions within which it has been conceived, each individual play or film may establish its own specific and individual sub-conventions that the audience must grasp in order to arrive at a complete understanding of what the performance 'means'. In Genet's *The Screens*, for example, the play's individual convention is that the characters themselves will paint an indication of the scenery on empty paper screens during the performance; in Peter Shaffer's *Black Comedy* he introduces the (originally Classical Chinese) convention that a lit stage means that the characters are in the dark and vice-versa; an adaptation of H. G. Wells's *The Invisible Man* might be based on establishing the convention that a character we can see, will in fact be invisible to the other characters on the stage. One could multiply these examples.

Such sub-conventions, specific to individual dramatic performances, must, of course, be learned by the audience during the performance itself. The author, the director and the performers thus have to develop techniques by which the action itself clearly teaches the audience the way they are supposed to 'read' these newly minted basic assumptions and technical devices.

5

To the many socially and culturally pre-determined conventions, assumptions, religious and moral beliefs, generic and technical pre-conceptions, we must add the personal store of assumptions and ideas, memories and expectations that each individual brings to a performance.

Important among these is the individual's own personal intertextuality: his or her previous experience of, for instance, performances of the same play by different actors, or individual actors' performances in other plays or films. In seeing, say, Olivier's Hamlet he or she may derive new and illuminating insights into the art of acting, and indeed the deeper meaning of the play itself by comparing this interpretation with different renderings of the role, previously seen, as for example holding Olivier's Hamlet up against the memory of Gielgud's or Scofield's account of the role.

The individual's interpretation of what he or she is seeing, the whole meaning of the performance will, in addition, be conditioned by a variety of factors inherent in his or her own personality: his or her visual sense and taste, say in clothes and furniture, personal preferences for certain physical types among the actors, or, indeed, specific personal interests. A professional historian will look at one of Shakespeare's history plays with a different eye than that of a non-specialist. A performance may contain signs that are obtrusive and pregnant with meaning to an individual spectator of which the originators of the performance themselves may have been totally unaware and which will remain unperceived by the rest of the audience. The story is told of an enthusiast who took his father, a dentist, to a performance of *Romeo and Juliet* only to elicit the comment that his father's main impression of the play was that the actress playing Juliet ought to have had orthodontic treatment when a child. A salesman at Miller's *Death of A Salesman* is said to have commented that he had always known that New England was a tough territory.

The barrage of signs emitted by the originators of the performance thus emerges in the mind of the individual spectator as an individually selected and hence unique cluster of messages and meanings.

As that worldly-wise practitioner, Goethe, saw it –

> Dann wird bald dies, bald jenes aufgeregt:
> Ein jeder sieht, was er im Herzen trägt.[3]
>
> [Then this or that will be aroused
> And everyone sees what he carries in his heart.]

Nevertheless, as we have previously postulated, at the end of a performance most, if not all, spectators will be able to agree on the basic *content* of the spectacle they have seen: that Hamlet was commanded to revenge his father's murder and was killed in the process, that the detective discovered the murderer, or that that charming doctor in the soap opera was indeed a golden-hearted gentleman.

This consensus must necessarily rest on the simplest, 'denotational' level of the signs perceived by the spectators. Once the more subtle 'connotational' aspects of the signs, sign systems and sign structures come into play perceptions and interpretations will begin to diverge: does Hamlet's black costume mean that he is in mourning, or that he is a melancholy person, or does his dressing in contrast to the rest of the court indicate that he is rebellious and wants to change the lifestyle of the country? And this oversimplified example deals only with a single item among many hundred possible perceptions that might influence an individual spectator's response.

6

Indeed, how many of the signs emitted in the course of a performance are actually perceived, and on what level?

The spectator of a dramatic performance, just like all of us in our daily lives, receives an almost infinite number of discrete sense impressions at every moment. Only a small fraction of all these perceptions can, of necessity, enter his or her full con-

[3] Goethe, *Faust*, Vorspiel auf dem Theater, lines 178–79.

sciousness. Hence the process of perception itself must be one of a constant selection and screening among the multitude of sense data we confront at any given moment. At any given instant during the performance the spectator's attention must be focused on the one or two elements among these hundreds of sense data that appear most essential.

Our perception of drama, as well as of the world itself, is thus 'intentional', directed towards the data we select for our conscious perception. The rest of the visual, aural, olfactory, tactile and other sensory fields of perception remains peripheral to our main focus of attention, but is perceived nevertheless, half-consciously or subliminally. Under hypnosis people who have witnessed a crime may be induced to reveal things they have perceived and stored in their memory without having been consciously aware of them.

In the same way a very large proportion of the signs perceived in the course of the performance of a play or film does not enter the consciousness but remains subliminal, just at or beyond the edges of the perceptual field, absorbed without actually becoming wholly conscious. Which does not mean that such perceptions are not powerfully effective. Indeed, it might be argued, that such half-consciously or subliminally perceived impressions are often more effective in influencing our reaction precisely because they remain outside our conscious awareness. They may determine the individual's selection of the unique cluster of messages and meanings which ultimately form his or her conscious awareness.

It is clear that a dramatic performance – being a mimetic representation of 'real' life, mirrors this state of affairs, but in an enhanced and, because more controlled and manipulative, intensified way. There will always be many more signs emitted by the performance than any individual spectator could ever wholly and consciously perceive or decode. Yet subliminally all these signs coalesce into the general impression, the mood and atmosphere, the 'feel' of a scene, a character or the entire film and play. A good director or designer will be aware of the power of all the subliminally perceived signs.

The shortest and most concise of all contemporary dramatic genres, the television commercial, provides the most striking illustration of this state of affairs, precisely because of its short duration. A thirty second commercial may only contain a few words of dialogue and minimal action, but it is crammed with half-perceived or wholly subliminal signifiers: the physical appearance of the characters, their clothes, the suggestion of their environment barely glimpsed in the background, the mood music or jingle, the colours, are here clearly all-important in establishing the attractiveness of the product that is advertised. Indeed, the action and dialogue which are consciously taken in by the audience can be regarded as merely providing the opportunity for unleashing the barrage of subliminal messages that are the really effective ingredients of the mini-drama. That the woman in the picture expresses satisfaction with the product is less important here than that she seems happy, beautiful, well-to-do, loved by her husband and family and deeply content with her life and thus transmits the strong implication that users of this product are destined for similar blissful felicity. In longer forms of drama the concentration of such subliminally perceived information may be less intense, and, indeed, a spectator who has more leisure to contemplate the set, the costumes and the general appearance of the characters is bound to become conscious of far more such signifiers. On the other hand the reflection, the subsequent 're-creation' of the story, the characters and the 'world' of the drama in the spectator's imagination, where the performance, the play, the film will manifest its ultimate 'meaning', will largely depend on the 'Gestalt' of these elements, arising out of a fusion of 'impressions' rather than on wholly consciously and discretely perceived details.

The process of communication involved in a dramatic performance thus can be seen as one of a continuous accumulation of consciously or subliminally perceived signifiers which are progressively synthesised, filtered and coalesced into more complex structures, which in turn are distilled into even more condensed, concise and generalised 'gestalts' out of which the ultimate, over-all 'meaning' of the drama will finally emerge. We are thus in the presence of a 'pyramid' of meanings. At its base there are all the multifarious individual signs, at its apex a complex but unified impression of 'what it was all about'.

Yet this general impression emerging from the synthesis of all the individual signifiers and strands and textures of signifiers, becomes in turn the basis of the widening circles of interpretations and thought processes to which a dramatic performance, if it has had a more than merely superficial impact on the individual spectator, may well lead as he or she reflects upon it.

With this we enter the field of the 'higher meanings' of aesthetic experience in general – and drama in particular.

XIV

A Hierarchy of Meanings

I

In Beckett's *Endgame*, at a certain point in the proceedings Hamm, the blind master sitting paralysed in his chair, becomes very alarmed. 'What's happening?' he asks his servant Clov. And Clov replies: 'Something is taking its course'. (That something is indeed the preordained course of the action of the play, which, once started, must relentlessly run through its fixed and repeatable structure in time.) But Hamm is alarmed. Terrified, he asks:

> We're not beginning to . . . to . . . mean something?
>
> CLOV: Mean something! You and I, mean something! (*Brief laugh*) Ah that's a good one!
>
> HAMM: I wonder (*Pause*) Imagine if a rational being came back to earth, wouldn't he be liable to get ideas into his head if he observed us long enough. (*Voice of rational being*) Ah good, now I see what it is, yes, now I understand what they're at!

Of course, being on a stage, Hamm and Clov *are* being observed by a crowd of presumably rational beings who are here being mocked because they will inevitably be asking themselves what the play they are seeing means, and who will go on thinking about that meaning later on, perhaps for a long time.

That, for Beckett, who feels that to ponder about the meaning of Life itself may well be wholly futile, is the ultimate paradox of drama: once we frame an image of Life by putting it on the stage or screen we are inevitably drawing attention to it as something to be looked at and scrutinised for what it means: even if, as in the case of Beckett's plays, the meaning the author might have wanted to express might merely be that it *has* no meaning.

For, if we look at a dramatic performance as an act of communication involving something that is being displayed to be looked at and hence a 'message' in the widest possible sense, something that someone wants us to see and know, conveyed by its originators to its recipients in a medium that is likely to transmit it to them, in a 'code' that they are deemed able to decode, then the recipients of what they must regard as being conveyed to them as something they are intended to 'take in' will inevitably look for the 'meaning' of that 'message'.

This is the case, even though drama, as we have seen, can hardly ever be reduced to a clear-cut personal statement by an individual creator, fully in control of the exact meaning of every element and sign contained in the message emitted. As essentially collective creations the dramatic arts are very different from those where an individual creator's conscious intention could indeed be postulated.

Even in those art forms, however, present critical attitudes do not attach undue importance to the author's intention. For one, that conscious intention might have had, underneath it, subconscious motivations; moreover, elements deriving from conventions that are taken for granted, rules that are being followed unquestioningly, a multitude of unspoken assumptions and traditions about technique and content, of which its author may well have been unaware, must have gone into the making of the work of art concerned. Hence it may well be the language, the technical traditions, the pre-existing formal rules of the art-form itself, rather than the individual author, that are making the statement.

In any case, once the poem, the novel, the painting, the

sculpture, is completed it becomes an autonomous artifact, open to any interpretation that a reader or viewer may bring to it. Any work of art, once it has left its creator's hands, is 'simply there', has entered, as Heidegger would put it, into 'Dasein' and has achieved independent being just like any other phenomenon of nature, a tree or a sunset, to be perceived and 'read' one way or another.

In the case of the 'performing arts', music and drama, the situation is even more complex. Insofar as a play or a piece of music has had an individual 'author' or 'composer' the completed script or score has become such a primary entity, 'there' to be read and interpreted. If it reaches the stage of being performed this primary 'given', however, passes through the process of being interpreted by another mind or minds who, in producing a performance, a recording, or a film, create a secondary artifact, a new and independent entity, which in turn will be something that is 'simply there' to be, in turn, open to any further interpretation or reading by its public.

In a dramatic performance, on the stage or screen, where the intentions, conscious and subconscious, of so many creative individuals have become fused, this secondary artifact will be further removed from the original author's intention than, say, in a musical performance where, through the greater precision of musical notation, the score prescribes the pace, rhythm and colour of each executant's contribution far more accurately. (And yet even in music individual performances vary widely, hence the great prestige of great conductors and soloists, their artistry and originality.)

The great complexity and fluidity of the interactions of different strands of creative contributions in drama, indeed, merely underlines its mimetic, representational nature. Drama is mimesis of life. And life itself, the interaction of human beings in their social and natural environment, is, after all, the product of an infinitude of individual circumstances, occurrences and intentions: so it is only fitting that its mimetic representation echoes that state of affairs.

Nevertheless that multitude of intentions is fused, in a dramatic performance, into a more easily apprehended, more intelligibly ordered and compressed form so that what may, at first sight, appear as an image of the amorphous 'reality' of life, society, the 'world', can actually aspire to make visible something of the underlying patterns of the forces that shape it, the order inherent in its rhythms of birth and death, meetings and partings, ascending and descending lines of life.

To attract their audience, to hold its attention, to express their view of the world, the originators of a dramatic performance must, of course, have had something in mind, something they wanted to express, to show, to demonstrate: a story to tell, an idea to embody. The individual signs emitted by the various participants in its creation may not be wholly harmonised, but in most cases they operate within a common, agreed structure of culturally based convention as to the significance of the signs deployed, and a consensus on the part of the originators of the performance as to the basic statement of the individual work on which they are engaged.

From the approximate consensus of the creative collective there will, if the collective itself is competent, result a consensus among at least the majority of their audience, at least as to the basic constituent events of the action they have been watching. They will agree that the hero got his girl, that the villain was foiled, that the murderer was caught, etc.

But that skeleton structure of the basic facts of the dramatic fable does not yet constitute anything approaching a full *meaning* of the performance. On that basis, for each individual spectator, there will arise a whole hierarchy of possible interpretations, reflections, insights which will, for him or her, ultimately, coalesce into something that will remain in his or her memory as a summed-up, encapsulated residue of what the performance 'was about', what it was trying to tell, what it 'meant'.

2

Yet, you may ask, does a dramatic performance, which in most cases is produced by its originators for profit and consumed by its recipients merely as a way to pass the time, necessarily have to have such a 'higher' meaning or moral content? Brecht spoke of drama that was mere pastime as being 'culinary' – that is: analogous to food which is consumed and passes through the body to be eliminated again at the other end – or, to put it more delicately: it goes 'in one ear, out the other'.

On reflection it can be argued that Brecht's analogy, in fact, tells us the very opposite: some of the food we eat does pass straight through, but some of it is incorporated into our system, sustains and even, ultimately, constitutes it: as the neat German pun has it: 'der Mensch ist was er isst' (man is what he eats). And it is precisely in this respect that the culinary analogy is very apt: even if no message or meaning of the performance, beyond its having helped to pass the time agreeably, is perceived, a residue of subliminal and subconscious meanings and messages remains: even the shallowest play, film, soap opera or situation comedy portrays and implicitly establishes patterns of cultural values (a happy love affair ends in marriage; crime does not pay; how does a strong man face adversity? how does a beautiful woman dress?) and thus drama establishes subconsciously held assumptions that shape the social mores and the behaviour patterns, implicit standards and role models of society. In fact, the less consciously these messages are perceived the more powerful – because totally unquestioned – is the impact of the value systems they represent. In that sense and on that level all drama is a purveyor of ideological and political messages, whether it openly questions the values of its society, or, what is so much more frequently the case, particularly in cinema and television, tacitly accepts and serves to reinforce them.

In establishing the hierarchy of meanings that drama can convey, therefore, we must be aware not only of the complex layers of meaning of those individual works that are original and notable enough to carry more or less profound individual messages, but also of the *cumulative* effect of the messages conveyed by the implicit assumptions carried by drama throughout its long history, whether these may have been religious, moral, political or merely behavioural.

Certainly the immense mass of dramatic material consumed in our own time each day by the populations of those countries that have reached saturation point in the provision of filmed or televised drama, has such an effect in shaping the value systems and attitudes of contemporary society.

There can be no doubt that, for example, television serials and 'soap operas' have become the most powerful purveyors of social values and philosophies, the objectives, the ultimate 'meaning' of existence for the large masses of the populations exposed to them. This is even more true of the most ubiquitous type of drama in Western societies – the television commercial.

The television commercial, in its concentrated and encapsulated form, exhibits in thirty seconds many features of the complexity of the hierarchy of meanings in drama. On the lowest level it very efficiently produces a consensus among the audience about what is happening (e.g. the conversion of the protagonist to the use of the advertised coffee, deodorant or detergent). It clearly states its immediate, consciously received message: Use brand X! But it also operates on the level of the reinforcement of an existing value system: the appearance of the people portrayed is calculated to evoke 'ideal types'. The briefly depicted, but subliminally perceived, environment in which they are shown also, cumulatively, over many such commercials, reinforces the model of the ideal home, its furniture and taste, the whole lifestyle it implies.

The immense number of such commercials the average viewer absorbs inevitably must coalesce into a powerful picture of the values of the society as a whole. And that picture, of course, is open to widely differing interpretations. While some members of the audience, though probably a minority, may perceive that cumulative picture of the society as an expression of an ethos of hard sell, greed, and preoccupation with the most trivial aspects of human existence, the vast majority will implicitly accept that subliminally imprinted image not only as that of unquestioned facts of life, but also as a model implicitly to be aspired to. In any case, whether these seemingly trivial mini-dramas build into an implicitly positive or a consciously analysed negative picture of the society and its values, they carry, over the long term, a powerful message, and can be seen as a potent cultural and political force.

This example, cited here without any polemical intention, merely because it is the simplest paradigm of a mostly much more complex state of affairs, can serve to illustrate how drama as a simulacrum of life and society holds as Hamlet says 'the mirror up to nature' and produces meanings on a multitude of levels: through the 'message' or 'moral' of a single performance of a play, film or television programme; as well as cumulatively through the subliminally absorbed implicit, unquestioned assumptions, that have emerged from the sum of many dramatic performances and shape the individual's attitude and opinions about society, human interaction, and the ultimate ethos of a given period; or indeed – in the very greatest drama – through the profound intellectual and social insights such a great work of art may have opened up.

3

It is the multiplicity of the sign systems it fuses together from the contributions of so many different artists and technicians that enables drama in performance to produce its peculiarly complete mimesis of 'reality'. For when confronted with drama, more so than with any of the other art forms, the spectator *has* to make his own sense of what he is shown. In most narrative fiction the author tends to provide his own commentary and evaluation of the events depicted. And painting and sculpture, however abstract, put before us what is evidently the artist's personal vision of the world.

Drama, that heterogeneous, impure art form, with its mixture of the earthy and the fictional, art and reality, is like Nature herself in its indeterminacy, in its really, or seemingly, value-free presentation of characters and events.

The author, the director and all the other artists contributing to the performance have abdicated their right to express their personal opinions. They have, in mimetically recreating the indeterminacy of the real world, shaped situations, characters, images that are open to a variety of different, even contradictory interpretations.

As nothing that a character says in drama can be taken to be its author's (or the director's or actor's) opinion but must always remain strictly only that particular character's view, it follows that the author's (or the director's) point of view, if such an expression of a moral or political attitude was, indeed, consciously intended, can only, ultimately, emerge as the resultant of the dialectical interplay of all the events, actions and opinions presented in the performance. Or rather: it should emerge from the very polyphony of its conflicts. And so, just as in real life each of us must arrive at his own assessment of events, the spectator of drama is compelled to extract his own value judgement, his own sense of what it ultimately 'means' from what he has perceived in the course of the performance.

Which is not to say that the creators of the dramatic event may not have had an opinion as to what they *wanted* it to mean, that they did not do their valiant best to manipulate and influence the spectators' judgement in the direction of that meaning. And here again, the best and most skilful practitioners will achieve a measure of success. The more so, the more they are aware of the precariousness of their endeavour.

The confluence of the intentions of all the various originators of the performance produces the dramatic event, which, in turn, should result in a consensus among at least the vast majority of spectators about what, basically, 'happened'. It is this consensual, agreed content of the action, however, which, in turn, must of necessity become the basis for the individual spectator's highly personal interpretation of what the performance 'meant' to him, and to him alone.

This is a process which begins during the performance but can, and frequently will, continue over considerable periods of time, during which the impressions consciously formed during the performance and the subliminal, or wholly unconscious, perceptions, moods, atmospheres, instinctual attractions and dislikes it has evoked, will gradually coalesce and develop, until, in the end, the memory of the experience consolidates itself into a lasting image or impression which becomes part of the individual's store of remembered experience that constitutes his or her personal inner world and contributes to her or his total, evolving, identity.

This distilled image and persisting memory of a dramatic event, however, is by no means unidimensional. It may well be present and active, simultaneously, on a variety of different levels.

4

It is this 'hierarchy' of meanings of which Dante, in a famous formulation of lasting validity, speaks in his letter to Can Grande della Scala, the tenth of his *Epistolae*, in which he dedicated his Divine Comedy to the ruler of Verona who had given him shelter in his exile, and gave an explanation of how he intended his poem to be read.

Here Dante indicates that the meaning of his work is not simple: 'quod istius operis non est simplex sensus, immo dici potest *polysemum*, hoc est plurium sensuum; nam alius sensus est qui habetur per literam, alius est qui habetur per significata per literam' (*Epistola X*, 7). (That the meaning of this work is not simple, but can be said to have multiple senses. For there is a difference between the literal sense on the one hand, and the meanings which are indicated by the literal sense on the other.)

Beyond the literal sense Dante distinguishes an 'allegorical or mystical', a 'moral' and an 'anagogical' sense inherent in his text.

He illustrates what he means by showing that the biblical story of the Israelites' flight into Egypt, can be seen 'literally' as a historical fact, 'allegorically' as an image of the redemption of mankind by Christ, 'morally' as an image of the transition of the soul from a state of sin to a state of grace, and 'anagogically' as signifying the eventual reception of the soul into eternal bliss.

This 'anagogical' meaning, which Dante elsewhere (in the *Convivio*) calls 'sovrasenso' – supreme sense – is the ultimate spiritual meaning that the reader can derive from the scriptures. In our context it is the highest form of spiritual or intellectual insight the spectator of a dramatic performance may experience.

But before that highest of all levels of meaning is reached there are the other 'higher' meanings inherent, and to be discovered by interpretation, in the 'text' or 'texture' of a performance (as in any other experience, literary, artistic or, indeed, 'real'): the allegorical and the moral.

For 'allegorical' we should today probably have to use expressions like metaphoric or symbolic, for 'moral' we might also put 'political', 'ideological', or 'social'. And there can be no doubt that any dramatic performance contains, and can yield, meanings at all those levels.

5

Metaphor and symbolism inhere in the very nature and fabric of drama. The stage, or the framed window of the screen, are themselves metaphors for the world – 'Bretter, die die Welt bedeuten' (boards that signify the world) as Schiller put it, while, as Shakespeare has it, the world itself can be seen as a metaphor for the stage. The stage or screen as a place where significant things are being exhibited elevates the most mundane objects and events to exemplary status, makes them significant beyond their mere individual being: they become signs for multitudes of similar objects and events: Romeo the exemplar of all lovers at first sight, Gregers Werle of all destructive fanatics of the truth, Miss Julie of all spoilt and restless young women. Any object, any gesture thus is potentially redolent of possible metaphorical and symbolic meaning, far beyond its literal or factual function in the performance.

To cite a simple example: in Chekhov's *Uncle Vanya* there is, so the stage directions tell us, in Vanya's den, where he runs the paperwork of the estate, on the wall a map of Africa. Now that map, which is only barely alluded to in the dialogue, has a very solid signifying function on the *literal* plane. It tells us that Vanya does not pay much attention to how his office is furnished: there could be more efficient tools on the wall of an estate office – for example output charts. The map is thus a very effective sign contributing to the delineation of Vanya's *character*. The fact that it is a school map, moreover, suggests that this room was originally used as the school room of the estate, where Vanya and his now dead sister received their tuition in geography and other subjects. It thus tells us a great deal about the *family history*.

Yet on the level of metaphor that map becomes a powerful sign for the absurdity of Vanya's existence, the incongruity of life itself.

On the factual level – a map of Africa. On the level of character an indication of Vanya's lethargy or indolence, on the level of plot an element of the family history, on the level of metaphor a symbol of the futility of human existence. All that in a single piece of stage property. Of course, whether all that is perceived by the individual spectator, depends on his or her mood and receptivity.

The metaphorical (Dante's 'allegorical') level thus elevates individual facts into general and generalisable perceptions about the nature of the world, life, the human condition and may produce profound insights.

Here, again, of course, drama merely mirrors the real world: if, in that real world, for example I meet another person for the first time, I have, on the basis of the signs he carries with him – appearance, clothes, speech, behaviour – to decide whether he is to be trusted, reliable, friendly or threatening, exactly as the spectator of a dramatic performance will decode the costume, speech, behaviour and appearance of one of the characters. But I can also see a person I meet as representative of a whole class of persons, as metaphoric for these or even of an abstract concept: the drunk in front of the Salvation Army shelter in the example used by Peirce and Eco stands for all drunks; an old man I meet in the street may become in my eyes a symbol for 'old age'; the postman who delivers a telegram may become the 'Angel of Death' if he brings the news of a dear one's demise; a sunset an intimation of mortality. Every object in the 'real' world thus has the potential of being perceived as a symbol, a metaphor. In the ordered, controlled and manipulated work of the signifying frame of drama this tendency of the 'real' to turn into the metaphorical is even more pronounced.

There have been periods in the history of drama when such metaphorical – and indeed allegorical – elements were central to the very style of presentation: the morality plays of the middle ages, or the allegorical masques of the Renaissance. But even in the realistic drama of our time – and in the even more realistic cinema – this dual nature of the real world continuously transforms even the most trivial objects into metaphors and symbols, simply because such objects – or characters – concentrate a multitude of meanings into themselves.

As the framed instrument for showing significant events, the stage or screen greatly enhances this tendency for people, objects and events in the real world to assume the quality of metaphors: it becomes itself a metaphor for the world: 'All the world's a stage'.

Shakespeare exploited this metaphoric nature of the stage in most subtle ways. If Macbeth compares man's brief existence in the world to a 'walking shadow, a poor player, that struts and frets his hour upon the stage, and then is heard no more' the metaphor is not only stated but incarnated by the actor who speaks it and who himself is a poor player who will be forgotten. He himself thus becomes the metaphor.

In a play by another – unjustly underestimated – Elizabethan dramatist, John Marston, *Antonio's Revenge*, there is a character, Pandulpho, an old man who throughout the first acts of the play has insisted on being a Stoic, hence unmoved by any misfortune.

Yet when his son is murdered, after at first attempting to appear unmoved, he does suddenly break down in tears. When challenged that as a Stoic philosopher he should not be subject to such emotion, he confesses:

> Man will break out, despite philosophy.
> Why, all this while I ha' but played a part,
> Like to some boy who acts a tragedy
> Speaks burly words and raves out passion;
> But when he thinks upon his infant weakness,
> He droops his eye. I spake more than a god,
> Yet am less than a man. (IV, 2)

This – that we are all like boy actors playing ancient heroes – is a moving poetic metaphor, but if one looks at the history of Marston's play and realises that it was written to be performed by the Children of St Paul's, one discovers that Marston was using a much more subtle type of metaphor: the old man talking about himself as a child actor playing a philosopher, *was* in actual fact a child. Here the actor not only used the poetic metaphor of the words of the text, he was that very poetic metaphor incarnated in a child acting an old man and drove home the basic insight that in our attempts to remain in control of our fate we are, in fact, all like child actors pretending not only to be grown up but wise old philosophers.

It is thus that the tension between the real actor and the part he plays itself becomes a powerful source of metaphorical meaning in drama.

Metaphorical overtones and meanings are inevitably present in all drama, even the most trivial-seeming. When I visited Czechoslovakia after the Russian invasion one of the leading Czech theatre men spoke to me of the difficulty they were having in avoiding being closed down for making anti-Russian statements. If they did Czech classics, that in itself was an assertion of their will to independence, if they did Western plays, likewise. So they felt the safest thing was bedroom farce. But then, when in one of the cliché farce scenes, the husband opened the cupboard and found the lover hiding there, the line: 'You have no business in my cupboard' brought the house down: the situation had become, in the eyes of the audience, a powerful metaphor for the situation of their country.

6

And that opens up the next level in the hierarchy of meanings, the one Dante labels the 'moral' one – which would nowadays include the social, political or ideological significances and overtones of drama. And as the anecdote from Czechoslovakia shows, this meaning can be totally independent from the intentions of the original author or, indeed, in this particular case, of the performers.

The 'meaning', or indeed the multitudes of meanings simultaneously perceived, or subliminally received, by the individual spectator of the dramatic action will always be the product of the interaction between the content of the signs it emits themselves, on the one hand; and the spectator's competence to decode them, on the other, and always, necessarily, in the context of his or her personal situation and the social and historical circumstances in which he or she finds him/herself. The same dramatic performance may mean one thing to a young person, another to an old one, and its 'moral', i.e. social, ideological or political meaning will powerfully depend on the social and historical context in which the performance takes place.

A performance of *Henry V* struck an English audience differently during World War II, when the country was embattled and in mortal danger (witness Olivier's film!) than it would today, when the martial rhetoric will sound entirely different in a world that has become as pervasively anti-militarist as our own.

Any drama whatever has political implications, simply because drama deals with human inter-action which, of necessity, must have its social and hence political aspects.

A play like *Waiting For Godot*, at one time much attacked in France for being non-political (and by implication, therefore advocating an attitude of political inaction, maintenance of the status quo and hence of a 'reactionary' *political* persuasion) assumed 'revolutionary' implications when performed in Algeria for landless peasants who interpreted the event awaited in vain as a metaphor for the promised but never fulfilled land-reform; in Poland the same ardently expected but never materialising event was seen as liberation from the Russians. Each different context produced different political, and now decidedly subversive, implications.

The further the author recedes in time, the less relevant become his original intentions, the more different will the 'message', what Dante calls the 'moral' meaning of the text, become.

A dramatic text must, thus, of necessity, be multivalent, synchronically by meaning different things to different individuals at any given moment; and diachronically, in the course of time. At one time and in one kind of society, Othello may have been regarded as guilty of marrying across the race barrier and thereby violating a moral law; at another time, and another place, he might have been seen as the innocent victim of wicked manipulation, and then again as a jealous sexist fool. And while in their own time and their own place these views may have been widely shared because of the political and social situation, some individuals in the audience may have derived radically different meanings from the events and characters in Shakespeare's drama.

A play like *The Merchant of Venice* was performed in Germany during the Nazi period as a vicious anti-semitic tract. The same play might be acted today as a celebration of the deep humanity of the Jews spurred to vicious revenge merely through their suffering under intolerable oppression and provocation. What Shakespeare himself and his company wanted to say with the play is impossible for us to tell, nor can it matter to the audience of a present-day performance.

The *Oedipos Tyrannos* of Sophocles was written for an audience in Athens who were not only familiar with the myth the play told, but deeply imbued with the religious connotations of such concepts as Fate, the will of the Gods, the truth of oracles etc. The same play still exerts a powerful impact on contemporary audiences: but clearly much of those original implications will be lost to them. On the other hand hardly anyone in an educated Western audience today will be unaware of Freud's concept of the Oedipus complex; they will primarily see the play as an illustration of that concept, of which the author, Sophocles, could not possibly have been aware. We may speculate about the reason that Sophocles could express something which was only formulated some two thousand years after him: we may say that in his unconscious the fear of incest was present, as it must be, if Freud is to be believed, in all human beings who have parents. Or we might say that the myth of Oedipus itself already contained this archetype of a collective human unconscious. But, ultimately, all this reasoning is irrelevant. *This* text has come to mean *this* to *us*. To future generations it may mean something completely new, and to us as yet unthinkable.

Drama, more than any other art, mirrors life; and in real life too we cannot say what the ultimate meaning of any event or experience we have undergone is or has been. An experience that seemed trivial today – let us say that of a girl being introduced casually to a young man – may later turn out to have been a decisive and happy moment in her life because later he became her husband. And another few years later, when they have split up, the meaning of the same incident will have turned into that of a disaster.

The great advantage of stage drama over the dramatic media that totally fuse text and performance – the cinema and recorded television drama – lies, precisely, in the fact that each performance can take the particular cultural, social, historical, geographical situation of its audience into account and adapt the basic content of the play to these changing circumstances.

In the live theatre, of course, the written portion of the play is merely a small part of the total 'text' or 'context' of the performance; here the director, the designers of set, costume, lighting, the musician and choreographer and the actors each contribute their individual signifiers. And their contributions will be different, and adapted to the taste, social and cultural, as well as technological conditions of their time, if and when the same text is staged in different countries and at different periods.

The cinema has been with us for too short a time to allow us to experience the change of meaning that a mechanically recorded and hence rigidly fixed performance text undergoes in time. Yet we can already see, in films that are half a century old, how radically the meaning of the performance changes for the eyes of a later generation: elements that were taken for granted – fashions in clothes or human appearance – now become powerful historical statements; social and moral assumptions underlying the action at the time the film was made, have become ridiculously stuffy or outmoded, elements that were highly original at the time (new techniques of montage, for example) have now become cliché and old-hat; the language itself has changed, what was up-to-date slang has acquired a period flavour; and so have the acting styles, etc. With this shift of viewpoint the value we may put on individual old films will also change: something that was unsuccessful when it was first made, will suddenly reveal important historical insights or be perceived as having been ahead of its time and hence important as a forerunner of present-day concerns.

7

That all drama, without exception, by its very nature, must carry powerful political implications and meanings – and that, at the same time, the originators of dramatic performance can never fully determine how their product will be interpreted at any given time and place by a multitude of individuals who come to the performance with widely different pre-conceived notions – produces the paradox of all ***political drama***, drama that has consciously and deliberately been conceived to achieve specific political or propagandistic objectives.

As all drama, necessarily, involves dialectical, dialogic situations, in which, as Hegel pointed out, each side must have, at least subjectively, strong arguments of its own and thus 'be in the right', it is difficult to manipulate the action in such a way that one side rather than the other will clearly be 'on the side of the angels'. Even in medieval allegorical drama the 'devil' often 'had the best lines' and emerged as the most popular character.

Too obvious a manipulation of the action to favour one standpoint rather than another will, moreover, be perceived by the audience and may well be resented by many individuals. Any too openly propagandist or ideologically biased drama may thus well turn out to have a self-defeating effect. The history of propagandistic theatre and cinema is rich in examples for this phenomenon.

Deliberately conceived political drama, nevertheless, can have a powerful political impact, provided the audience already brings a pre-disposition towards its message to the performance. This is particularly true of patriotic, national drama:

Henry V in England, *Wilhelm Tell* in Switzerland; Mickiewicz's *Forefathers' Eve* in Poland, and it is equally true of revolutionary drama: the great masterpieces of early Soviet film fall into this category. Yet these instances tend to confirm the view that drama is not a very good vehicle for the propagation of specific ideological views. These plays and films preached, and still preach, to the converted.

Thus, on the whole, drama may not be very effective in achieving short term political objectives. In the long term, on the other hand, it has been and remains a powerful influence on changing social attitudes, on the gradual development of the collective consciousness. It is not the direct appeal, the surface message that is most effective, but, in keeping with the essential nature of the dramatic, the indirect implications of the dramatic action, the meaning that emerges, as it were, between the lines of the dialogue, from the wider reverberations of the action.

It is an oft repeated assertion that the performance of Beaumarchais' *Marriage of Figaro* at the Comédie Française in April 1784 played an important part in making French public opinion ripe for the French Revolution. If that is so, the political impact of the play was a very significantly indirect one: it merely showed a servant who was not only intellectually superior to his master (that had been a commonplace of comedy from Plautus to the *commedia dell'arte*) but could be seen actively resisting his master's aristocratic pretensions and winning against him (rather than putting his wit at the service of his master's intrigue).

Similarly the impact of the naturalistic drama of playwrights like Ibsen, Hauptmann, Gorky or Shaw, which contributed a great deal towards changing public attitudes to women, the working classes, sexual mores, etc., was a gradual and indirect one. Drama tends to exercise its most powerful and lasting moral impact by reflecting the attitudes of the more advanced groups among the population, exposing them to public outrage and discussion and thus gradually penetrating the consciousness of society. The process is one of a continuing circle of feedback: changing views in society reflected in drama, in turn change the moral climate of society and prepare the stage for the next phase of change that will, in turn, again eventually be reflected in drama, and so on and on.

The gradual humanisation of attitudes towards racial and sexual minorities, the opening up of hitherto taboo subject matters to public discussion that has characterised the development of the last fifty years in Western society has owed a great deal to drama on stage and screen.

Yet this influence towards change that the leading edge of the dramatic media displays has always to be seen against the background of the equally indirect and much more powerful impact of popular drama in re-inforcing the political, moral and social *status quo*.

8

The social and political impact of drama used – in the past – to be regarded as springing from its being experienced by a crowd of human beings assembled in one room and forming a temporary collective entity: a crowd, an audience.

In an epoch where most drama is experienced by the largest masses of people in isolation or small groups in front of television sets, this connecting link to the sources of dramatic experience in tribal or social and religious ritual is far less apparent.

Indeed, it remains somewhat of an open question whether television as a dramatic medium is, in fact, capable of producing the most intense – anagogic – experiences and meanings at all, simply because it lacks the 'mysterious' ingredient by which, at the highest peak of artistic, emotional and intellectual intensity, the collective fuses into a higher entity and partakes in a quasi-mystical moment of insight. In fact, in the sober light of reflection that mysterious element is simply an aspect of 'mass-psychology', as outlined by Le Bon or Freud, the outcome of the heightened concentration that springs from the individual's awareness of the other spectators' attentiveness, their bated breath, their stillness, or, conversely their wild laughter and manifest enthusiasm.

There can be no doubt that the most deeply felt and most intensely remembered experiences of dramatic performance derive from this mass-psychological situation of the individual spectator who feels his or her personality merge into a trans-personal presence, becoming one with the collective personality of the crowd. It is at such moments, rare though they may be, that drama exercises its maximal impact and is capable, as both Brecht and Artaud postulated, of changing the individual's attitude to life, of giving him or her lasting spiritual and intellectual insights.

Nevertheless, however deeply and intensely enhanced the individual's experience of a higher, spiritual, 'anagogical' meaning of the dramatic event may have been, there can be no such thing as a collectively perceived 'meaning' that would be truly common to all those present. The intensity of concentration, perception, emotional impact may certainly have been heightened by an awareness of similar concentration and emotional intensity in the other members of the crowd, but the 'content' of what is so intensely experienced, the 'meaning' of the dramatic event, will, of necessity, remain strictly the individual's own, his specific private experience.

And basically that individual's experience is the point at which all the efforts of the creators of dramatic performance, all the signs and sign systems they have deployed, must reach their destination and final effect.

The meaning of such a dramatic performance on the highest plane, its impact, message and their ultimate distillation into that individual's store of memory or attitudes to life depend on that individual's personality, background, knowledge, prejudices and preferences as much, if not more so, than the intentions of the author, director, designers, musicians, or actors who originated the event.

Whatever they intended to convey is transformed and translated into that individual's personal impression and experience. There can be no 'correct', 'final', 'ultimate' or 'true' interpretation, no pure, 'metaphysical', 'Platonic idea' of the ultimate meaning of a dramatic *text*, and much less so of the infinitely more complex texture of a dramatic performance.

There can be agreement, by exact analysis, of what happens in the dramatic 'text' and 'texture' on the purely factual denotational level, there can be debate on the moral, philosophical and poetic implications of that text and the manner in which it was presented in an individual performance. And these will necessarily change in the course of time, simply because not only do the conditions under which the drama itself is seen alter, but because previous critical interpretations – and previous practical interpretations by previous directors and actors – subtly change the starting point for the audience that comes to it aware of those interpretations.

In the cinema, where that whole texture of the performance is permanently fixed, the meaning of that fixed artifact will itself change in the course of time and under the influence of an accumulated body of interpretation and opinion that will have accrued around the work, provided it was important enough to have had a lasting impact.

In the theatre where only the verbal text is permanent and can be re-incarnated in an infinite number of different productions, that process is even more variable and complex. Every *Lear* that follows Peter Brook's *Lear* will contain its influence, or react against it – and there will be spectators who come to it with that previous experience and knowledge and will see it in the light of it.

The more complex, the more multi-layered and subtly structured the perception of a dramatic performance becomes for the individual spectator, the higher its artistic, philosophical, moral – anagogical – impact will prove; the less possible will it become to arrive at an exact, 'scientifically' valid determination and analysis of its 'meaning'. And the phenomenon at its highest point of intensity and complexity merely highlights what is the case even on its most basic level. The ultimate meaning of a soap opera (because so much is subliminal) is as impossible to reduce to a scientific formula as the most subtle work of a Bergman, Mnouchkine or Fellini.

9

Drama is a mimesis of real life. But the book of nature is not written in a language that can be codified in a dictionary or a grammar. There are so many meaning-producing systems at work there that any moment of experience is abundantly over-determined and ambiguous. There is no fixed code in reality, hence the theatre cannot be reduced to a fixed system of codes either.

The theatre is a simulacrum – at its highest level, ordered and elevated to the status of art – of the real world and real life. That is why Antonin Artaud called his book *The Theatre and Its Double*. The theatre – as the other forms of drama – is too complex to be capable of being reduced to a language with its predetermined rules of grammar and signification. Although drama uses many languages and signifying systems, it is the double of life itself, a controlled, simplified double, but a double nevertheless.

That is why on any level, but especially on the highest plane of the hierarchy of meanings, the anagogic, a dramatic performance transcends any attempts at being reduced to anything so mundane as a single definable and generally valid meaning.

It can have such a meaning, or many meanings on many levels, for individual audience members. But over and beyond that, if it reaches that level, it will achieve something much more subtle and much more profound: over and above its message or messages, its different levels of meaning, it may be able to give its audience, each individual in it, differently, an *experience*, on both the emotional and intellectual planes, which in the course of two or three hours will concentrate into that span of time what would be the emotional experience and the intellectual lesson of, say, a whole love affair, or any other decisively formative episode of an individual's life.

In that sense there is more to drama than mere communication. True, a communication takes place, an ultimate residue of meaning is left behind for the individual spectator, all the codes, all the signifiers are in operation and can be analysed ad infinitum, but what really matters in the end in such a dramatic performance is that the spectator should emerge having had an emotional, poetic and intellectual experience of an intensity and significance perhaps as great, perhaps even greater than one of the pivotal, decisive experiences of his or her 'real' life. That is what Artaud meant when he dreamt of a theatre that would shake its audience to the very core of their personality.

This is the manner in which drama can truly enhance our existence and can play an immensely valuable part in enriching our world, extending the scope of our experience and our understanding of the human condition.

Such is, of course, the ultimate highest level of the impact of all the arts – the point at which an aesthetic experience can approach the intensity and transforming power of a religious experience. But drama, particularly those forms of it that are witnessed by a mass of spectators, so that one individual's experience is enhanced and multiplied by the experience of all the others, is particularly able and predestined to produce experience of overwhelming intensity and profundity. Hence the often stressed affinity between drama and ritual – and the use of dramatic forms of expression in ritual, as, indeed, the use of ritualistic forms in drama.

The ability and the power of drama to create an emotional experience of the utmost intensity, akin to religious or mystical ecstasy, an experience that may become a climactic turning point in an individual's life, and transform that individual, or conversely a deeply unsettling experience like that which Hamlet inflicted upon his uncle, is the true measure of its importance in the fabric of our lives, our society and our culture, the true extent of the 'very cunning of the scene'.

Bibliography

J. Dudley Andrews, *The Major Film Theories. An Introduction*, Oxford: Oxford Univ. Press, 1976

Lisa Appignanesi, *The Cabaret*, London: Studio Vista, 1975 (2nd ed. London: Methuen, 1984, N.Y: Grove Press 1985)

William Archer, *Play-Making. A Manual of Craftsmanship*, Boston: Small, Maynard, 1912

Michael Argyle, *Bodily Communication*, London: Methuen, 1974

Michael J. Arlen, *Thirty Seconds*, N.Y.: Farrar, Straus & Giroux, 1980

Rudolf Arnheim, *Film as Art*, London: Faber & Faber, 1958

James F. Arnott, Joelle Chariau, Heinrich Huesmann, Tom Lawrenson, Rainer Theobald, *Theatre Space. An examination of the interaction between space, technology, performance and society*, Munich: Prestel, 1977

Odette Aslan (ed.), *L'Art du Théâtre*, Paris: Seghers, 1963

Antonin Artaud, *Oeuvres Complètes* (Nouvelle édition revue et augmentée) Vol. I – XXI (being continued), Paris: Gallimard, 1976 – 1986 –

— , *Collected Works* (tr. V. Conti), 4 vols. London: Calder & Boyars, 1968–74

—, (ed. Susan Sontag) *Selected Writings*, N.Y.: Farrar, Straus & Giroux, 1976

John L. Austin, *How to do Things with Words*, London: Oxford Univ. Press, Cambridge, Mass.: Harvard Univ. Press, 1962

— , *Philosophical papers*, (Third Edition), Oxford: Oxford Univ. Press, 1979

Denis Bablet and Jean Jacquot, *Le lieu théatral dans la societé moderne*, Paris: Centre National de la Recherche Scientifique, 1963

Béla Balázs, *Theory of the Film*, London: Dennis Dobson, 1952
Roland Barthes, *Elements of Semiology*, London: Cape, 1964
—, *Système de la Mode*, Paris: Seuil, 1967
—, *Essais Critiques*, Paris: Seuil, 1964
—, *L'obvie et l'obtus. Essais Critiques III* Paris: Seuil, 1982
—, *Le bruissement de la langue. Essais Critiques IV* Paris: Seuil, 1984
—, *L'Empire des signes*, Geneva: Skira, Paris: Flammarion, 1970
—, *Le grain et la voix. Entretiens 1962 – 1980* Paris: Seuil, 1981
George Pierce Baker, *Dramatic Technique*, Boston and N.Y.: Houghton Mifflin, 1919
André Bazin, *What is Cinema? Essays selected and translated by Hugh Gray*, Berkeley: Univ. of California Press, 1967
Walter Benjamin, 'Das Kunstwerk im Zeitalter seiner technischen Reproduzierbarkeit' in *Schriften*, vol I, Frankfurt: Suhrkamp, 1955
Jonathan Benthall and Ted Polhemus (eds.), *The Body as a Medium of Expression*, London: Allan Lane, 1975
Gianfranco Bettetini, *Produzione del senso e messa in scena* Milan: Bompiani, 1975
Günter Bentele (ed.), *Semiotik der Massenmedien*, Munich: Ölschläger, 1981
Marshall Blonsky (ed.), *On Signs*, Baltimore: Johns Hopkins Univ. Press, 1985
Bertolt Brecht, 'Schriften zum Theater', vol. VII (hardback), vols 15–17 (paperback) of *Gesammelte Werke*, Frankfurt: Suhrkamp, 1967
—, (ed. & tr. John Willett) *Brecht on Theatre*, London: Eyre Methuen, 1964
J. S. Bruner, A. Jolly and K. Silva (eds.), *Play – its Role in Evolution and Development*, London: Penguin, 1976
Paul Bouissac, *La Mesure des Gestes. Prolégomènes à la sémiotique gestuelle*, The Hague and Paris: Mouton, 1973
Elizabeth Burns, *Theatricality: A Study of Convention in the Theatre and in Social Life*, London: Longman 1972
— and Tom Burns, (ed.), *Sociology of Literature and Drama*, London: Penguin, 1973
Roger Caillois (ed.), *Jeux et Sports*, vol. XXIII of *Encyclopédie de la Pléiade*, Paris: Gallimard, 1967

Marvin Carlson, *Goethe and the Weimar Theatre*, Ithaca and London: Cornell University Press, 1978
—, *Theories of the Theatre*, Ithaca and London: Cornell University Press, 1984
Jean Cazeneuve, *Les Rites et la condition humaine*, Paris: Presses Universitaires de France, 1958
J. L. Davitz, *The Communication of Emotional Meaning*, N.Y.: New York Univ. Press, 1964
Etienne Décroux, *Paroles sur le mime*, Paris: Gallimard, 1963
John N. Deely, (ed.) *Tractatus de Signis. The Semiotics of John Poinsot*, Berkeley: Univ. of California Press, 1985
John Deely, Brooke Williams and Felicia E. Kruse (eds.), *Frontiers in Semiotics*, Bloomington: Indiana Univ. Press, 1986
Jacques Derrida, *L'Écriture et la différence* Paris: Seuil, 1967
—, *De la grammatologie*, Paris: Ed. de Minuit, 1967
—, *La Dissémination*, Paris: Seuil, 1972
Denis Diderot, (ed. F. C. Green), *Writings on Theatre*, Cambridge: Cambridge University Press, 1936
Friedrich Dürrenmatt, *Theater-Schriften und Reden*, Zürich: Arche, 1966
—, *Dramaturgisches und Kritisches. Theater-Schriften und Reden II*, Zürich, Arche, 1972
Guy Dumur (ed.) *Histoire des spectacles*, vol XIX of *Encyclopédie de la Pléiade*, Paris: Gallimard, 1965
Jean Duvignaud, *Sociologie du théâtre. Essai sur les ombres collectives*, Paris: Presses Universitaires, 1963
—, *L'Acteur. Esquisse d'une sociologie du comédien*, Paris: Gallimard, 1965
Umberto Eco, *A Theory of Semiotics*, Bloomington: Indiana University Press, 1976, London: Macmillan, 1977
—, 'Semiotics of Theatrical Performance' in *The Drama Review*, No. 21, N.Y.: 1977
—, *Travels in Hyper-Reality. Essays*, San Diego, N.Y. London: Harcourt Brace, 1986
—, and Thomas E. Sebeok (eds.), *The Sign of Three. Dupin, Holmes, Peirce*, Bloomington: Indiana Univ. Press, 1983
Michael Egan (ed.), *Ibsen: the Critical Heritage*, London and Boston: Routledge and Kegan Paul, 1972

Keir Elam, *The Semiotics of Theatre and Drama*, London & N.Y.: Methuen, 1980

Martin Esslin, *Brecht – A Choice of Evils*, (4th ed.) London & N.Y.: Methuen, 1984

—, *An Anatomy of Drama*, London: Temple Smith, 1976, N.Y.: Hill & Wang, 1977

—, *Artaud*, London : Fontana, 1976. N.Y.: Penguin, 1977

—, *Mediations. Essays on Brecht, Beckett and the Media*, Baton Rouge: Louisiana State Univ. Press, 1980, London: Methuen, 1981

—, *The Age of Television*, San Francisco: W. H. Freeman, 1983

Erika Fischer-Lichte, *Bedeutung. Probleme einer semiotischen Hermeneutik und Ästhetik*, Munich: H. C. Beck, 1979

—, *Semiotik des Theaters. Eine Einführung*, 3 volumes, Tübingen: Günter Narr Verlag, 1983

John Miles Foley (ed.), *Oral Tradition in Literature. Interpretation in Context*, Columbia: University of Missouri Press, 1986

Gustav Freytag (ed. E. J. MacEwan), *Technique of the Drama*, Chicago: Scott, Foreman & Co., 1900

F. W. Galan, *Historic Structures. The Prague School Project, 1928 – 1946*, Austin: Univ. of Texas Press, 1985

Wolfgang Gersch, *Film bei Brecht*, Berlin: Henschel 1975

Gilles Girard, Real Quellet, Claude Rigault, *L'Univers du théâtre*, Paris: Presses Universitaires de France, 1978

Erving Goffman, *The Presentation of Self in Everyday Life*, N.Y.: Doubleday Anchor Books, 1959

—, *Ritual Interaction: Essays on Face-to-Face Behavior*, N.Y.: Doubleday Anchor Books, 1967

A. J. Greimas, *Sémantique structurale*, Paris: Larousse, 1966

—, *Du sens*, Paris: Seuil, 1970

Henri Gouhier, *Le Théâtre et l'existence*, Paris: Vrin, 1980

Georg Friedrich Hegel, (ed. A. & H. Paolucci), *Hegel on Tragedy*, N.Y.: Doubleday Anchor Books, 1962

André Helbo, *Les Mots et les gestes. Essai sur le théâtre*, Lille: Presses Universitaires de Lille, 1983

— (ed.), *Sémiologie de la représentation. Théâtre, Television, Bande dessinée*, Bruxelles: Editions Complexe, 1975

Andrew S. Horton and Joan Magretta, *Modern European Filmmakers*

and the Art of Adaptation, N.Y.: Frederick Ungar, 1981
Roman Ingarden, 'Von den Funktionen der Sprache im Theaterschauspiel' in *Das Literarische Kunstwerk* (2nd. ed.), Tübingen: Niemeyer, 1960
Aloysius van Kesteren and Hertha Schmid (eds.), *Moderne Dramentheorie*, Gronberg/Ts.: Scriptor Verlag, 1975
—, *Semiotics of Drama and Theatre. New Perspectives in the Theory of Drama and Theatre* vol 10 of *Linguistic and Literary Studies in Eastern Europe*, Amsterdam/Philadelphia: John Benjamins Publ. Co., 1984
Mary Ritchie Key (ed.) *Nonverbal Communication Today. Current Research*, Berlin, N.Y., Amsterdam: Mouton, 1982
Tadeusz Kowzan, *Littérature et Spectacle*, The Hague and Paris: Mouton, 1975
Siegfried Kracauer, *From Caligari to Hitler: A Psychological History of the German Film*, Princeton: Princeton Univ. Press, 1947
—, *Theory of Film: The Redemption of Physical Reality*, N.Y.: Oxford Univ. Press, 1960. (English ed.: *Nature of Film*, London: Dennis Dobson, 1961)
—, *Kino: Essays, Studien, Glossen zum Film*, Frankfurt: Suhrkamp, 1974
Franz H. Link, *Dramaturgie der Zeit*, Freiburg: Rombach, 1977
Georg Lukács (ed. F. Benseler), *Emtwicklungsgeschichte des modernen Dramas*, Darmstadt and Neuwied: Luchterhand, 1981
Marshall McLuhan, *The Gutenberg Galaxy*, London: Routledge and Kegan Paul, 1962
—, *Understanding Media: The Extensions of Man*, London: Routledge and Kegan Paul, 1964
Gerald Mast and Marshall Cohen, *Film Theory and Criticism: Introductory Readings* (3rd ed.), N.Y. and Oxford: Oxford Univ. Press, 1985
Ladislas Matejka and Irwin R. Titunik (eds.), *Semiotics of Art. Prague School Contributions*, Cambridge, Mass.: MIT Press, 1976
Christian Metz, *Film Language. A Semiotics of the Cinema*, N.Y.: Oxford Univ. Press, 1974
Vsevolod Meyerhold (ed. E. Braun), *Meyerhold on Theatre*, London: Methuen, 1969

Jean Mitry, *Esthétique et psychologie du cinéma*, 2 vols., Paris: Editions Universitaires, 1963 – 1965
Georges Mounin, *Introduction à la sémiologie*, Paris: Ed. de Minuit, 1969
A. M. Nagler, *A Source Book in Theatrical History*, N.Y.: Dover, 1952
Horace Newcomb (ed.), *Television: The Critical view*, 3rd ed., N.Y. and Oxford: Oxford Univ. Press, 1982
Bill Nichols, (ed.) *Movies and Methods. An Anthology*, Berkeley: University of California Press, vol. I, 1976, vol. II, 1985
Laurence Olivier, *On Acting*, London: Weidenfeld & Nicolson, 1986
Patrice Pavis, *Dictionnaire du Théâtre*, Paris: Éditions Sociales, 1980
—, *Problèmes de Sémiologie Théâtrale*. Montréal: Presse de l'Université de Quebec, 1976
—, *Voix et Images de la Scène. Essais de Sémiologie Théâtrale*, Lille: Presses Universitaires, 1982
—, *Voix et Images de la Scène. Pour une Sémiologie de la Réception* (new and revised edition of above), Lille: Presses Universitaires, 1985
—, *Languages of the Stage. Essays in the Semiology of Theatre*, N.Y.: Performing Arts Journal 1982
Charles S. Peirce, *Philosophical Writings* (ed. J. Buchler), N.Y.: Dover, 1955
—, *Selected Writings (Values in a Universe of Chance)* (ed. P. H. Wiener), N.Y.: Dover, 1958
Stephen C. Pepper, *Aesthetic Quality. A Contextualist Theory of Beauty*, N.Y.: Scribner, 1938
John Poinsot, *Tractatus de Signis* (see Deely)
Georges Polti, *The Thirty-Six Dramatic Situations*, Boston: The Writer, 1960
Vladimir Propp, *Morphologie du conte*, Paris: Seuil, 1965
Barry Salt, *Film Style and Technology: History and Analysis*, London: Starword, 1983
Ferdinand de Saussure, *Course in General Linguistics* (1916), London: Fontana, 1974
Dieter Schwanitz, *Die Wirklichkeit der Inszenierung und die Inszenierung der Wirklichkeit*, Meisenheim am Glan: Hain, 1977
John R. Searle, *Speech Acts. An Essay in the Philosophy of Language*,

Cambridge: Cambridge Univ. Press, 1969
Theodore Shank, *The Art of Dramatic Art*, Belmont, California: Dickenson, 1969
Kaja Silverman, *The Subject of Semiotics*, N.Y. and Oxford: Oxford Univ. Press, 1983
Etienne Souriau, *Les deux cent mille situations dramatiques*, Paris: Flammarion, 1950
Bert O. States, *Great Reckonings in Little Rooms. On the Phenomenology of Theater*, Berkeley: University of California Press, 1985
Victor Turner, *From Ritual to Theatre, The Human Seriousness of Play*, N.Y.: Performing Arts Journal Publications, 1982
— , *Dramas, Fields and Metaphors: Symbolic Action in Human Society*, Ithaca and London: Cornell Univ. Press, 1974
Anne Ubersfeld, *Lire le théâtre*, Paris: Editions Sociales, 1977
André Veinstein, *La mise en scène théâtrale et sa condition esthétique*, Paris: Flammarion, 1955
Ludwig Wittgenstein, *The Blue and Brown Books*, Oxford: Blackwell, 1958

Index